IN THE IMAGE OF PETER

MARK: The Man and His Message

IN THE IMAGE
OF PETER

MARK: The Man and His Message

by

E. M. BLAIKLOCK

M.A., LITT.D.

Professor of Classics, University of Auckland

MOODY PRESS

CHICAGO

Printed in the United States of America

CONTENTS

		Page
PREFACE	. . . .	7
THE YOUNG MAN MARK	. . . . .	9
THE UNPARDONABLE SIN	. . . .	22
THE MAN FROM THE TOMBS	. . . .	40
PARTY AT MACHAERUS	. . . . .	51
ON THE MOUNTAIN AND AFTER	. . . .	62
THE MAN WHO TURNED AWAY	. . . .	77
CLIMBING WITH CHRIST	. . . .	88
THE HINGE OF HISTORY	. . . .	98

PREFACE

HOW THIS BOOK WAS BORN

The following pages are not a commentary on the Second Gospel. The reading of the sombre chapter of Tacitus on the Great Fire of Rome turned me to the closer reading of the little book which that event, I believe, indirectly inspired. That was in the winter of 1962. A remark of a member of my staff, Dr. H. R. Minn, also caught my attention, and I read the Greek text of Mark with renewed interest.

In the Christmas vacation of that same year I was invited to speak at Pounawea, the world's most southerly Christian Convention. I spoke on the Gospel of Mark. The story began to live, as I read and studied the text, with that strange power and intimacy which stamps a book as a classic, the utterance of conviction, and the truth. When I was invited to give the Bible Readings at Keswick, during my sabbatical leave of 1964, I had no difficulty in choosing a subject. The book was still alive in my experience. Hence the form of the chapters which follow. They are themes which emerged vividly from the Gospel. They were designed to prompt wider study, for the book itself, I was sure, was of vastly greater importance than anything I could say about it.

But the terse and hasty pages of Mark will always be tangled in my mind with the roar of the mighty surf of the South Pacific, crashing on the world's ultimate shore, where the Catlins and Owaka rivers join by the moa-

hunters' camp at Pounawea, or with the sheen of Derwent-
water, and a smudge of rain in the jaws of Borrowdale.
And among the people I have learned to know in Mark's
story, will move those we met in the old manor on the hill
where Skiddaw rises blue above the rose-garden.

Pounawea and Keswick seem very far away as these
words are written a few months later. Philadelphia lies
wide below the tall apartment house. Penn stands high on
the City Hall, and the endless traffic swirls along the
Schuylkill Expressway. But is not one of the lessons of the
Gospel of Mark the unity of all Christians in Christ?
Leagues and centuries may divide, but the Person in whom
we live and move and have our being draws us all very
near to Himself and to each other.

September 20, 1964.   E.M.B.

THE YOUNG MAN MARK

Mark 1. 1–8; 14. 43–52; Acts 12. 12, 25; 13. 5, 13;
15. 38, 39; II Tim. 4. 11; Philem. 24; I Pet. 5. 13;
II Pet. 1. 15, 16.

THERE is profit and sometimes warning in some of the
shorter biographies of Scripture. Enoch is the subject of
one challenging verse, Demas of another. Mark's story,
like that of Apollos, may be culled from a dozen verses.
John Mark, Mary's son, nephew of the gracious Barnabas,
Peter's friend and convert, the friend Paul lost and found
again, the missionary who failed and tried again, comes
very close to us in those few brief references.

Perhaps we meet him first as a 'teen-age' boy, the lad who
was present at the arrest in Gethsemane. Imagination must
aid the terseness and obscurity of the text, but was this the
untold story? . . . In the long room on the roof of the house
of Mary, the rich widow lady of Jerusalem, the Lord and
His band meet for what was to be the Last Supper. In his
room below, awake and alert, for he sensed the danger
which lurked about the house, lay Mary's son, John Mark.
He heared the hurried steps of Judas on the stairway without, and listened with sharper care. And then the noise of
feet, and the rest depart.

On a sudden impulse the boy seizes a linen sheet from
his bed, wraps it round his body and follows. He watches
under the olive trees, sure that some crisis is at hand. A
flare of torches, and the betrayer is there. With a boy's
reckless loyalty he shouts some protest, and angry hands
lay hold of him. Slipping out of his sheet Mark escapes.
Perhaps he bore a cruel and mutilating sword-slash across

his fingers, for an old tradition says that in the early Church Mark was called 'the Stumpfingered.' Shall imagination be followed a little further? Did the savage blow and the cry of his young friend stir Peter to draw his long fisherman's blade and slash back at the offender?

The Unsuccessful Missionary

The facts are more certain when next we meet Mark. It is perhaps fifteen years later. With Paul and Barnabas, John Mark has reached Perga, a port of Asia Minor. Suddenly, and for no reason stated in the text, Mark leaves the party. Mark's reason must have angered and disappointed Paul, for some years later, when Barnabas sought to include his relative for a second missionary journey, a 'sharp contention' rose between him and Paul, and the two great men parted.

Scripture is frank but reticent of detail. One fact, however, emerges with a painful clarity. In the judgment of Paul, Mark had failed. He was an unsuccessful missionary. What stumbled him? It is probable that he failed to share a vision which had taken shape in Paul's mind. The apostle had been deeply moved by the response of the Governor of Cyprus to his message. He himself was a citizen of three worlds, a Jew, a Greek, a Roman in one. Again and again we see Paul pass with ease from one role to another. At Perga can be seen the first forming of a plan. He may have had more than one reason for the long journey inland to Antioch of Pisidia. A malarial attack, perhaps his 'thorn in the flesh' could have prompted the hasty departure to the high country beyond the ranges. But also Antioch was the chief centre of Roman power in mid-Asia Minor.

The whole pattern of Paul's ministry begins here. He offered Christ to Rome. He sought with political acumen to plant the faith in key towns, strategic bases of empire. Rome rejected Christ, and in that rejection Paul was to die fifteen years later, but this is not to say that he was misguided. Did the young Jew in the party think that he was wrong? Was national prejudice so strong in him that he refused to be party to Paul's move into the Gentile world? Prejudice and pride can work hand in hand and destroy fellowship and usefulness. Was Mark in Perga simply because a mother's or an uncle's ambition was determined that the young man should be a missionary? A parent's folly can lead to such disaster. A parent's one duty is by all means to bring a child to Christ, to guide humbly, and prayerfully advise, but for the rest to be uncommitted.

Paul's Sorrow

Was Paul right in standing firm? Events vindicated him. There was trouble enough in Antioch, Iconium, and Lystra. A member of the party whose heart was in the synagogue, and who was not prepared, when rejected by the Jews, to turn to the Gentiles, would have been a burden indeed. Gideon found it better to face the raiders from Midian with three hundred alert men who set comfort second, and drank from their hands with eyes warily on the hostile farther shore, than with the thousands whose hearts were not wholly on the task. God can do nothing with the lukewarm. He likened Laodicea to the sickly, soda-laden water which flowed in a tepid stream past the town. Christ promised fulfilment only to those who hunger and thirst after righteousness. Mark, if we have read the story aright, could have been no help in Asia. It was better for him to go.

But the 'sharp contention' with Barnabas left a mark of sorrow on Paul's mind. The word used by Luke is *paroxusmos* from which we get the word 'paroxysm.' Signi-

ficantly enough, when Paul wrote for the Corinthians his
great poem on love, he remarked, as our common version
has it: 'Love is not easily provoked.' It is moving to note
that the verb Paul uses is *paroxunetai*, the verb which corre-
sponds to the sad noun in the story of Paul's dispute with
Barnabas. In the eloquence of that chapter, he was painting
a picture not of himself but of his Lord. He wrote that
phrase and used that word with emotion and self-reproach
behind his pen. The sharp edge of vehemence in tongue or
pen returns too easily to cut the one who uses it. 'Love is
not sharp-tempered', and a serene and quiet mind is the
last fruit of the grace of God.

So Paul rejected Mark. God had not rejected him.
Fundamentally Paul was right, if wrong in his sharpness.
And Mark was wrong. In Christ, for all that, failure is not
final. The harsh appraisal of men, even of good men, is not
always that of God. He does not quench the smoking flax.
Mark failed because he was in the wrong place. Qualities,
wrongly employed, become defects. Paul once likened the
Church to a body complete with limbs and organs. Hand
cannot function as foot, nor heart do the work of lungs.
Tension invades the community of Christ when people try
incongruously to function in ways for which they have no
aptitude or calling. In a healthy body each member per-
forms harmoniously its allotted task. So in the body of
Christ. Each must do his proper work or become a liability.
Mark was impulsive, hasty, perhaps too vehement. Those
very qualities were to make him successful in the real task
which awaited him, the writing of his terse, brief Gospel.
Paul wrote of the body of Christ in Chapter Twelve of his
first letter to Corinth. Perhaps he thought of Mark, his
hasty dismissal of one as hasty as himself, and of events
which followed, and which were to restore their fellowship.

The Other Friend

Bewildered and hurt, Mark went off to Cyprus with Barnabas. And perhaps that gentle relative was the first to see that at this stage the mission-field was not Mark's calling. Another friend was at hand to show what his real vocation was. It was Peter, in whose active mind, over those darkening years while Paul was in prison at Caesarea and Rome, a conviction was growing. Consider the circumstances . . . in July, A.D. 64, nineteen centuries ago, Rome burst into flame. For a long and awful week fire raged through the capital, and an enraged people sought a scapegoat. Nero, the young emperor, was in fact blamed, rightly or wrongly no one will ever know. Certain it is that the burning of a slum-ridden Rome made room for the vast, mad building schemes which Nero had in mind. And rumour had it that, seeking poetic inspiration in the awful sight, Nero had stood on an eminence, watched the sea of flame beneath, and sung of burning Troy with lyre in hand. Lyre changed to fiddle, he has passed into a trite saying for orators and politicians.

Such rumours were dangerous, and Nero was afraid. At this point some scoundrel drew his attention to an aloof minority, the Christians. Did they not hate society and abstain from its pagan activities? Had they not talked of a day of judgment, and fire on a guilty world? Here was a scapegoat, made possible by popular contempt for a tiny band who stood apart from society's wickedness, and challenged sin by their stern righteousness. Nero turned on them, and persecuted them with such hideous cruelty that Rome's own hardened proletariat turned at last in disgust from his savagery.

Thus, in the panic act of a sadist, began Rome's long folly of persecution. At some point in the next few years

Rome made its choice. Paul's vision faded. It was to be Caesar, not Christ, and vast historical consequences flowed from that rejection. Had the Empire accepted Christ in the days of its strength, and not in its decline, all history might have been different. Had multitudes turned to a healthy, simple Christianity, had authority refrained from base policies of persecution, the ills of slavery and the power of the army, which destroyed the Empire, might have been undermined. Had a vigorous evangelism, from a Europe so strengthened, spread a message of peace to the barbarian world, there might have been no collapse of ancient civilization.

There were enlightened minds which saw this tragedy afar off. When Paul saw the passing of his hopes we do not know, but there is a sentence in Peter's second epistle which may mark the point for his brother apostle. Somewhere early in the sixties of the first century, Peter noted the hostility which was to erupt in persecution. 'I will endeavour,' he wrote, 'that you may be able after my decease to have these things always in remembrance. For we have not followed cunningly devised fables when we made known to you the power and coming of the Lord Jesus.' He saw the need for a written record, and in this expression of the need was in all likelihood the beginning of Mark's Gospel. Mark was Peter's son in Christ, and Peter's influence is so pervasive in the book that Justin half-a-century later called the book the 'Memoirs of Peter.'

But note this significant fact. Mark wrote for the Roman world. He had followed Peter's difficult road, and come to see that, whatever the outcome, the Gospel must be offered to the Empire. He was taking up the task he abandoned at Perga, and forwarding it more effectively than he could have done by remaining the junior attendant on Paul and

Barnabas. Paul recognized the fact, and renewed affection followed. In Mark's Gospel, therefore, we meet the man who failed and tried again, the man who, by a friend's help, rebuilt a testimony, and left that testimony in a deathless book.

You can do nothing more useful than to make time to read that book, and to read it again and again, in all available versions, in any language you know, in the Greek in which Mark wrote it if you can. You can read it in an hour, aloud in under an hour and a half, and the simple text of the book matters more than anything which anyone can say about it. There most intimately you will meet Mark, businesslike, terse, clear. There, too, you will meet Peter, Mark's father in Christ, so human, lovable, weak and yet triumphant. There you will meet the first Christians. . . .

You will find them curiously modern, for the events of Mark take place daily around us. Let me illustrate that statement, for I want you to read with awareness a tale, indeed of the first century, but full of the twentieth, of men and women in a remote and alien world, but one full of the human problems of today, near, and true to our experience. . . . Five years ago I was in Corfu, and one afternoon we visited Palaeokastritsa, a beautiful bay on the island's lush western coast. Here it was, according to the people who live there, that Odysseus of the ancient story swam ashore from his wrecked ship. The local patriots point to three rock pools down the coast where the princess Nausicaa, as Homer tells, did her washing, and met the weary hero who was hiding his salt-caked, battered person in the scrub. And an island off the shore is, they say, the ship in which the kindly king sent Odysseus home to neighbouring Ithaca. In anger, the sea-god Poseidon, says the legend, turned it into stone.

Now Lawrence Durrell, the writer, lived at Palaeo-kastritsa, and in his charming book on Corfu, *Prospero's Cell*, he tells the story of which my remark on Mark's Gospel reminded me. Next door to Lawrence Durrell lived a workman, Anastasius, and one night the English author was aware of late hours in his neighbour's small cottage. The oil lamp burned on and on, and there was a sound of laborious reading aloud. In the morning Durrell saw Anastasius with a crumpled paper-covered book. He was full of a story they had read in it, about one named Odysseus, who had fought his way home from Troy through manifold disaster. The book was a primer from the local school, which little Sky, the labourer's daughter, had brought home. So work-filled had been poor Anasta-sius' youth, that he had never heard of the great Greek hero, and the famous tale of Odysseus had hit the family, unspoiled by television, radio, and a plethora of cheap books, like something magical from another world.

Anastasius was amazed that his English neighbour knew the tale. Durrell proceeded to explain: 'When Odysseus reached here from Fano . . .' he began. 'Reached here, *here*?' said Anastasius in bewilderment. 'Do you mean it happened, and it was *here*, in Corfu?' 'Yes, yes,' said Durrell, 'do you know the first of the three bays before the hotel in Palaeokastritsa? It was there that he met the prin-cess. And King Alcinous had his palace under yonder olive grove.' (There is a grey-green clump of old olives on a neck of land by the beach.) Anastasius was overwhelmed. 'It is very strange,' he said, and hurried home delighted, the battered book in his hand. His familiar landscape had sprung to life when he found that an old story was still real, its events all round him. Something like that is true of the New Testament. Like Anastasius's story of the old Greek hero, the story of Mark's Gospel is alive in our own landscape, its people curiously like ourselves.

First Christians

Look at them. The first disciples, first members of the band who were to change the whole course of history, were fishermen from the Lake of Galilee. They were moderately prosperous men, for their trade was rewarding, the chief industry in one of the most thickly populated parts of the Middle East. They gave up a comfortable livelihood when they followed Christ, but they were men who had been stirred by the message of the desert preacher, John. Revival had swept the land when the fiery prophet of the Jerusalem wilderness rose in protest against the corruption of established religion. John died a violent death, as Christians still die under tyranny today, because his fearless voice lashed a ruler's sin. It is the old shame of man to rise and beat down in malice that which challenges and rebukes sin. His Galilaean converts went back to their active and rewarding calling. But nothing, as the Mongol proverb has it, returns as it was, and perhaps they were not surprised when the call to other service came. It had its price, and Christ still asks, as He asked of John's disciples who became His, that advantages be put second, and material things held with a light hand by those who give Him their devotion.

They were a varied group, like those who read these words. There was Peter, a born leader, impetuous, bold, a man of action. There was Simon the Zealot. The nickname indicates that Simon had been a passionate nationalist. Palestine was occupied territory, and no people bore such bondage as hardly as the Jews. The Zealots were the terrorists of the Jericho road, the murderers of Roman

B

soldiers. Simon found the purpose he sought, and calm for the wild hatreds which tore him, in allegiance to Christ. At the other end of the scale was Matthew, the tax-collector. He was a cynical collaborator with authority, a man who, for easy gain, had allowed himself to become part of the system of tyranny. No one knew the self-loathing in the man's heart, the secret aspirations for better living. Christ saw them, and Matthew was called from the tax-collector's desk to write the first book of the New Testament, and live a gloriously useful life. Had Simon met Matthew on the Jericho road in the days before both met Christ, the Zealot would have readily killed the collaborator. They became one in Christ.

Mark plunges into his theme, by-passing the stories of Bethlehem and the Nativity on which Matthew and Luke dwell so exquisitely, like a man in haste to have his say, as though time were limited. Christ himself moves into the narrative within three hundred words from its beginning. He calls His first disciples. He moves through the crowded towns of Galilee, preaching, and as Edward Vernon's attractive translation of the book puts it, 'driving away the Evil Things that afflicted men's minds'. He is shown among the outcasts, the scorned and rejected, giving healing and hope.

Opposition gathers. The Gadarenes bid Him depart. He had healed a man's mind of wild delusion, and in the process interfered with business in a vicious little town. The people of Gadara preferred their corrupt ways and their material advantage to a healthy-minded community, and urged Christ to go. The corrupt priesthood did more. He had cleansed the Temple of the racket which filled the sacred court with hucksters and money-changers bringing advantage to the priests, and from that moment the plot began to destroy Him.

Christ knew it and faced it. He began to warn His un-comprehending disciples, and there are awesome pages in the story which speak of the Lord's steadfast march to the Cross. He faced, open-eyed, betrayal and violence. He faced it all because there was no other way to reveal to rebel man the ghastly tragedy of his sin, and the glory of the love of God. Try to imagine an alternative, a Christ striking down His foes, a Christ compelling man's surrender. It is impossible to think of it. But Christ crucified daunts our hearts, and brings us to His feet. The Cross shows us what we are, and the horror of rejection in which the evil of the human heart ends. It leads us to cry for forgiveness, as though in that timeless, ancient crime we all were and are involved. 'We were there when they crucified our Lord.'

But the Cross was not the end. Christ rose from the dead. That fact above all others makes the Gospel of Mark a real and living story. The tale of the betrayal, the trial, and the death, is real and modern enough, for men still abandon truth and righteousness for thirty pieces of silver, and betray Christ in hypocrisy. Justice is still perverted, truth is still upon the scaffold, and wrong upon the throne. Good men are still lost in the noisy, vicious crowd, their protest dumb upon their lips and silent before a multitude clamouring for evil. A few still stand by the cross, fearlessly true to their faith. It is all part of a too familiar scene. But above all, the little book is real because Christ still lives.

Mark drew his story from Peter, so ancient tradition says, and Peter looked into the empty tomb, and talked with the risen Christ in the dawn on the beach. So sure was Peter, that he died for his faith in Rome about the time Mark wrote his Gospel. He was crucified upside down. Men do not face a ghastly death like that for a lie or a legend. Mark

himself probably died not long after. We think that he was
in Rome about A.D. 67, and it was a dangerous time to be
there, with the Rome of Nero's last mad days decimating
the Church. The Gospel seems to have been finished in a
hurry, the last verses being perhaps by another hand. Read
the closing page with reverence, and pause at the end of
verse 8, for it is possible that Mark ended his writing at that
point. . . . The clash of grounded spearbutts in some Roman
courtyard, the harsh battering on the door, the hasty
thrusting of the hurried last pages of the Gospel into concealment—and the end. . . .

The Fruit of Such Study

Mark's Gospel can do much for us as we read it again.
Note its first words, the first words of the story of Christ
ever to be read aloud before a Christian congregation. To
be sure there were letters of Paul and Peter already in the
possession of the Church, but here was a Gospel, the first of
the famous four. '*Arche tou euangeliou Iesou Christou* . . .'
came the words in the lilting accented Greek. . . . '*Princi-
pium evangelii Jesu Christi* . . .' would come the Latin rendering for the few who knew no Greek. . . . 'The beginning of
the Gospel of Jesus Christ . . .' we read today in countries
where the legions never marched.

And in those very words there is an element which
eludes us. 'Gospel' meant 'good news', and that was a fair
rendering of the Greek and Latin words. . . . 'The Good
News of Jesus Christ begins thus . . .' might be a fair translation, and good news it was to fear-ridden pagans and law-
ridden Jews that the debt was paid, and man was redeemed.
Catch that note as you read the familiar words again. May
it come as good tidings that the man who falls can rise
again, that if one path ends in frustration and defeat another

can open to most glorious success; good news that man is not left to struggle alone, but that One is here to aid, to sustain, to cleanse, and to keep; good news that there is rest in Him, fulfilment, a rock to stand upon, healing for heart and mind, the banishing of fear, and above all forgiveness.

Let this book fuse, complete and warm our fellowship. . . . In his charming book, *Sons of the Generous Earth*, published early last year, Philip Oyler tells the story of a visit he paid to a recluse in rural France. It was a simple bare cottage, a wooden table, a wooden bench, a built-in wooden bed with a covering of sheepskins. The mantelpiece over the open fireplace was a sort of altar. A crucifix stood there and a beautiful reproduction of Leonardo's head of Our Lord, the one with the closed eyes, for Leonardo was humble enough and sensitive enough to realize that no artist could catch on canvas the light and mystery of those eyes. And there too lay a well-thumbed book.

When his host left the room on some errand outside, Oyler's curiosity overcame him and he satisfied his curiosity about the book on the mantelpiece. It was a worn and well-read copy of the Gospels in Greek. When the good man returned the visitor asked him whether that was his whole library. But let Philip Oyler tell the story in his own words. . . . 'He said that it was, and that he could read it over and over again, and on each occasion he was given to see more in it than he had ever seen before. I put my hand in my pocket and drew out of it a very well-worn copy of the same book and showed it to him. Tears filled his eyes as they met mine, and we embraced in silence, for how could spoken words avail? We were aware of our affinity, and we knew that He who rules the planets leads, too, our human hearts to Him and to one another.'

THE UNPARDONABLE SIN

Mark 2. 23-36; 3. 22-30.

THE sombre and solemn warning which forms the substance of the verses in this reading, is a climax in Mark's story. In this Gospel the plain reader gains the clearest and the readiest conception of the chronology of the Lord's ministry. But consecutive though the narrative appears to be, incidents and groups of incidents are recounted with the same disproportion of space as in the other Gospels. Mark, like his fellow evangelists, had an end in view. The major theme in all of them was the story of one week, and its consummation in the death of Jesus Christ, and His resurrection.

Hence the rapid arrival at the first clash with evil, which foreshadowed that end. Chapter One sketches in swift words the days of popularity, and the Lord's ministry throughout the Galilaean synagogues. It was a mission whose success and frustration were embedded in the parable of the sower and the seed of Chapter Four, but there had been sufficient popular acclaim to stir the attention of the Pharisees of Capernaum. They appear in Chapter Two, dissecting the Lord's words, critical, hostile. The days of the happy, popular ministry in the little towns are over. Evil has rallied, and the entrenched pundits and dignitaries, who found religion the natural sphere for their pride, love of position, and self-interest, were organizing against the intruder.

In Chapter Three they show their hand. Embittered over

the Lord's sane contempt for the clutter of their Sabbath rules, the local Pharisees took counsel with the Herodians. This was a sort of Society of Friends of Herod, a corrupt group dedicated to bolstering the puppet ruler and to forwarding his interests, no doubt in promotion of their own. Wickedness is abroad, full-sized and sinister. The rejection of the Lord is already real. The seeming triumph of His foes is in clear view.

The Lord turned from them to organize the Twelve, the splendid project of the assault on the world. Rejected in one place, it is always well to turn to another. He commanded as much, and led the way. Meanwhile the Capernaum Pharisees went to work. They invited some of the leading members of the sect from Jerusalem. The deputation came, studied the situation, and passed their verdict. It was shocking. 'He casts out devils by the prince of devils.' In a few trenchant phrases the Lord dismissed the illogical proposition: 'How can the devil fight against himself? If a country fights against itself it cannot last long. If the inmates of a house turn against each other the family will break up.' He went on: 'But now let me tell you very solemnly: People will be forgiven all kinds of wickedness, even the vilest sins and the unholiest talk, but to call the goodness of God the work of the devil, and to call God's Spirit an evil spirit, is a sin past forgiving.' (Verses 24, 25, 28, 29: Vernon's paraphrase.)

So came into Scripture the Unpardonable Sin to which John mysteriously refers in the last pages of the New Testament to be written. It is our chief theme today, a theme rich in popular misunderstanding. It can be understood only in its context, and part of the context is this sequence of events, and the persons who, in the Lord's stern and devastating word, had so sinned and destroyed themselves.

The Pharisees

Who were the Pharisees? The name means 'the Separated,' and appears in history about 135 B.C. They do, however, represent a movement much older in time. People sometimes realize the value of the good things they have only when they lose them. That is true of individual men and women. It is true of nations. It was true of Israel. Carried into captivity by the cruel deportation policies of the Babylonian kings, Israel turned to her ancient faith. The Temple, and its associated patterns of worship, were gone. The Law remained, and became an enthusiasm with those who refused to conform to the shape of pagan life. There were two types: those who like Daniel stood out, those who like Esther conformed. From the Daniels descended the Pharisees. They preserved the Jewish faith, the Jewish sense of nationhood. The Esthers and Mordecais became 'the Lost Tribes.'

Like many magnificent spiritual movements among men, the Pharisees began in ardour, faith, and dedicated enthusiasm. They did fine work. And like many movements they degenerated, became proud, separated, not from compromise and paganism, which was the first significance of their name, but from the common people whom they should have led and helped. 'This crowd, that knoweth not the Law, is accursed,' said the Jewish Sanhedrin. The preservation of the Law became at last an end in itself, and not a means to a greater end. The explanations, comments and refinements of keeping the law proliferated like healthy cells turned cancerous, and destroyed the body of which they formed a part. The better members of their order retained grace and scholarship, and sought justice and truth. Nicodemus and Gamaliel must not be forgotten. Nor must the fact that Paul speaks with pride of having been a

Pharisee. The lesser members of the order, and the majority, perhaps, of the six thousand which they numbered in the time of Christ, were self-righteous legalists, the butt of the Lord's terrific denunciation in Matthew's Gospel, the breed who hesitated to stand on the polluted floor of Pilate's court, lest they be defiled for the Passover, but were there for no other purpose then to lie, bear false witness, and do an innocent man to foul and agonizing death. A righteous enthusiasm, a beneficent pursuit, turned inwards, turned sour, corrupted by self-esteem and pride, and forgetting its one purpose, produced a moral catastrophe.

The Sabbath

The Pharisees' enthusiasm for the Sabbath, the occasion of their first clash with Christ, is an illustration of their perverted zeal. Their passion for organizing the Law, and burying Moses under a mountain of legalism, had, indeed absurdities enough in other spheres. The Sabbath was prime illustration. The only knot, for example, which a Pharisee could tie on the Sabbath day, was a knot which could be tied with one hand. One could knot a belt in the interests of preserving the effectiveness and purpose of one's clothes. Therefore it was possible to lower a bucket into the well on the Sabbath day, provided one used a belt, and not the customary rope. There was a catalogue of thirty-nine works not to be done on the Sabbath. Digging was one, but do not imagine that digging meant simply spading the earth. To drag a chair along the ground was prohibited, lest it make a rut, and seed be fortuitously sown. If one's house burned, one could not carry garments out save those actually worn. But outside one could strip and return through the smoke any number of times to secure another load actually worn.

The provision is typical of the 'escape clauses' which the Pharisees invented to make life possible, and to circumvent their own legislation. The limit of a Sabbath journey, for example, was about two-thirds of a mile. If, however, one desired to travel farther, it could be made legal by depositing food for two meals at the boundary of one day's journey on Friday. This made the boundary technically or legally 'home,' and another journey could be undertaken. An egg laid on the Sabbath was taboo. But simply express the intention on Friday of one day roasting or potting the hen, and the egg became a mere part of a legally dead bird, which had fallen off, and could be eaten.

Two illustrations were in today's reading. One Sabbath, towards the close of the first year of His ministry, the Lord was passing with His men along the path which commonly led through the cornfields. It was the 'hard ground' of the parable of the sower, the beaten track on which inevitably some of the scattered seed fell. The grain was ripening and the hungry disciples took and rubbed out some ears in their hands, eating as they walked. This was not theft. It had the sanction of the Deuteronomic law. But it was the Sabbath. Technically the men were both reaping and threshing. The Pharisees were loud in protest. They had been waiting for this occasion of rebuke.

The Lord replied ironically on the level of their understanding. He charged them with ignorance of the Scriptures. In hunger David once doubly violated the Law. He was a layman, but intruded into the shrine. He ate the consecrated bread, which only the priests might eat. This constituted precedent for legal minds. A more pertinent instance was the Temple. On the Sabbath the priests slew the sacrificial victims, and did much other work. This was not reckoned impiety. 'I tell you,' said Jesus, 'something greater than the Temple is here.' He meant Himself, and it was inevitable that His hearers would remember that at the previous Passover He had cleansed the Temple and called it His Father's house.

This was gall to the Pharisees. On another Sabbath the Lord was in the synagogue when a man approached Him with a withered hand. According to one of the apocryphal gospels he said: 'I was a mason, winning a livelihood with my hands. I ask you, Jesus, restore me to soundness, lest I have the shame of begging for food.' Only when life was in danger did the Pharisees permit healing on the Sabbath. They watched. The Lord brought the man forward. 'Is it lawful to do good on the Sabbath?' He asked, 'to save life or to kill?' It was a skilful question, for the rabbis had decreed that if a beast had fallen into a pit on the Sabbath, the owner was to ascertain whether it was hurt. If not, he was to feed and bed it but not extricate it until the next day. If it was hurt, he was to get it out and kill it. This was difficult and wasteful, so they had an escape regulation. The owner could get the beast out of the pit with the announced intention of killing it, and then not do so. In other words, they could twist their own laws for an animal but not for a man.

Hypocrisy

All this sophistry was too serious to be merely ridiculous. The Sabbath was invented as a humane and beneficent institution. In the hands of the first legalists it became a fanaticism. In Chapter Two of the First Book of the Maccabees, that brave tale of the Jewish resistance movement against Syria, the story is told of the massacre of a thousand unresisting Jews, who would not repel attack on the Sabbath. Significantly, the leaders took counsel, and in the same chapter a decision is recorded to resist in future such attacks, but to take no offensive action.

This was the principle which, by the first century, had run wild. To make life possible amid the tangling and frustrating mass of their prohibitions, a corpus of such subterfuges had corrupted the character of their inventors. Hypocrisy was spawned amid such legalized dishonesties, and standards of uprightness undermined. Hence the Lord's scorn and terrific denunciation in the long speech recorded by Matthew. He could not abide, as He cannot abide, sham, smooth deception, the evasion of justice, of purity and truth, duplicity and hypocrisy. The Pharisees are a solemn warning, for their breed is not dead.

Some principles in fact emerge to be conned and studied by those who shun hypocrisy. Let five be listed. First, let it be realized that religion can be horribly correct in all its outward forms, postures and observances, and lack the spirit of Christ. Secondly, religion can be very preoccupied with doctrine, and tolerate sin. Character and conduct are the recognizable fruit of correct doctrine. Thirdly, religion is not divorced from common sense. The splendid sanity of Christ pervades the Gospels. The Lord's answer to the Pharisees was always compounded with simple, sturdy common sense. Fourthly, religion is for all, not for the initiated *élite*. The last books of the Bible to be written, John's Gospel and his first Epistle, were produced to rebut the first attempt within the Church to do what Pharisaism had done in Judaism, to corner religion, withdraw it from common men, make it the possession and prerogative of the chosen, a mystic cult understood only by the enlightened. Fifthly, religion is something which enlarges life, enlivens body, heart, and mind, invades beneficently, not restrictively, all activity, and takes life and personality over, not to cabin and confine in regulation, but to expand, liberate, and beautify. The Chapel of Christ and Industry in Coventry Cathedral has a round altar. It faces all directions. It is approachable from all angles. So is true religion in the life of any man.

It is the eternal preoccupation of evil to drain off spiritual energy, ardour, and enthusiasm into side issues, externals, irrelevances, to adulterate devotion, and sidetrack zeal. This had happened to the Pharisees. In the vast baptistry of St. Sophia at Istanbul, the huge stone basin has a snake carved round its outer edge. There lurks Satan, on the lip and edge of the act of surrender and consecration, to corrupt the zeal, poison the effort, and enfeeble the strength of the new life. 'It is Christianity AND, which we must encourage,' writes the Senior Tempter in C. S. Lewis's amusing and instructive *Screwtape Letters*, 'Christianity and anything at all as long as it is not pure Christianity.' So it is visible all round us—Christianity *and* Pacificism, Christianity *and* the Ecumenical Movement, Christianity *and* Denominationalism, and so on. With the Pharisees it was the worship of God *and* legalism, nationalism, sectarianism ... until truth was lost, zeal was perverted, pride grew big, strong, and tyrannous, and the end was crime unspeakable, murder, blasphemy, and damnation.

The portentous hypocrisy of Pharisaism can arise again. Wherever a movement begins in goodness and sincerity, outlives usefulness, and degenerates into a set of postures and attitudes, the ugly heresy is abroad again. Let everyone beware of putting loyalty to sect or denomination before the wider loyalty the Christian owes to Christ. Wherever habits of piety lose their inner urge and meaning, grow rigid and 'mark a wind of yesteryear,' the peril of Pharisaism looms. Whence my phrase? In Réné Bazin's beautiful novel *The Dying Earth*, the decay of the French country-side is studied. The old château whence the marquis had once ruled his rustic tenants is in decay. The heir has gone to Paris, and the old rooms are cobwebbed and the drives and gardens a tangled wilderness. And on the tower 'the weathervane, rusted stiff, marked a wind of yesteryear.' Churchgoing, Bible-reading, prayer itself? Do they mark the urge and vitality of today's devotion, or are they the surviving habits of more dedicated and warmer-hearted days, the remnants and surviving scraps of truer loyalty?

Yes, and wherever ambition, self-seeking, pride, love of place and position, pomposity, intrigue, the search for advantage, greed for reward, lying, insincerity, the jealous propagation of man-made rules, exclusivism, and cold-heartedness invade the holy place, there is Pharisaism. It is vicious, evil, unchristian.

The Unpardonable Sin

Hence the terrible words of the Lord's warning. We must deal with it frankly. What is 'the unpardonable sin'? False notions are abroad, and a certain type of evangelism is not without its share of blame for that. Towards the close of an evangelistic campaign it once was the fashion to sing Mrs. Alexander's unfortunate hymn:

> There is a line by us unseen
> Which crosses every path,
> The hidden boundary between
> God's patience and His wrath.

For myself I prefer: 'Loved with everlasting love.' But be that as it may be—the evangelist then read from Deuteronomy 1, how 'they came to Kadesh-Barnea,' hesitated again, and were forbidden to enter the promised land. 'As

for you get ye into the wilderness, by way of the Red Sea.'
The spiritual, nervous, mental damage done by this shocking and unscriptural teaching was terrible.

Let the ground first be cleared by asking what 'the unpardonable sin' is not. It is not exhausting the love, grace,
and patience of God. 'Whosoever cometh unto me,' said
Christ, 'I will in no wise cast out.' Both of the available
Greek negatives are used in the verse. It is impossible to
make a more emphatic negative assertion. 'If anyone, anyone at all, at any time, with any past, from any sin, comes in
penitence to me, I will not under any conceivable circumstances turn that person away.' Can a promise be more
absolute? Could it have been made by One more utterly
true?

Nor is 'the unpardonable sin' any one of the common
sins which damage, mar, and ruin human life. The list of
the forgiven is evidence enough. Jacob was a liar, a swindler,
a deceiver of his aged father, greedy, treacherous. In
wrestling and turmoil of soul, he found his peace with God.
David was an adulterer and a murderer. The heart-broken
penitence of Psalm 51 was not rejected. Matthew and
Zacchaeus were cynical traitors, collectors of dishonest
money, cruel, extortioners. They could have been nothing
else as part of the tax-machine. They entertained Christ.
One of them was an apostle. He wrote the first book in the
New Testament. The Prodigal Son wasted a fortune in
carnal sin. He was heartless, unfilial, weak. His father killed
the fatted calf for his returning. The thief on the cross was a
terrorist, a man of violence and blood. Christ welcomed
him to Paradise. Peter denied his Lord with oaths of curs-
ing. He was recommissioned. Paul was a rabid persecutor
of good men. He stood and watched a martyr die. He was
forgiven.

Or would you look at 1 Corinthians 6. 9-11? Here is
J. B. Phillips's rendering:

> Have you forgotten that the Kingdom of God will never
> belong to the wicked? Don't be under any illusion—neither the
> impure, the idolater or the adulterer; neither the effeminate, the
> pervert or the thief; neither the swindler, the drunkard, the
> foul-mouthed or the rapacious, shall have any share in the
> Kingdom of God.

Is 'the unpardonable sin' one of this list? It is a sharp and
drastic word. But the passage continues:

> *And such men, remember, were some of you!* But you have
> cleansed yourselves from all that, you have been made whole in
> spirit, you have been justified before God in the Name of the
> Lord Jesus and in His very Spirit.

Out of all these sins is the Prodigal's way. God remembers them no more. 'Though your sins be as scarlet,' runs a
verse in the chapter of Isaiah already quoted, 'they shall be
white as snow.' And Isaiah had in mind the deep scarlet,
shot with purple, which the Phoenicians made from the
juice of the murex shellfish of the Palestine coast, a colour
which impregnated the tissues of the garment beyond all
possibility of washing away. God forgives, and will always
forgive when sin is brought to him in confession. Carry its
burden no more.

What then is the blasphemy against the Holy Spirit
which the Lord declares is beyond forgiveness? It must be
sin which is not confessed and brought penitently to Him.
The New Testament does not contradict itself, and only
thus can its verdicts on forgiveness, the forgivable and the
unforgivable be reconciled.

Consider it thus. This is the process of God's dealings

with man. The Holy Spirit prompts men to consider Christ. The effect is an overwhelming consciousness of inadequacy. 'Depart from me,' cried Peter when the awareness of Christ's glory broke on him, 'for I am a sinful man.' Christ does not depart. He draws near when the heart is anguished thus. Penitence follows, and forgiveness.

But reverse the process. Dogged refusal to listen to the promptings of the Holy Spirit, in pride of heart or nourished hatred, results in an inability to see the beauty and challenge of His perfection. That inability stifles all sense of sin. The sinner so paralysed cannot repent. He cannot therefore be forgiven. It is self-willed hardness, not a form of words, which constitutes blasphemy against the Holy Spirit.

This was the situation with the Jerusalem Pharisees on their visit to Capernaum. They identified Christ's work with the Devil's work. They declared in measured and deliberate terms that the healing He had brought to tormented lives was the activity of evil powers. To lie thus, thus to misrepresent and corrupt goodness and truth, was to demonstrate evil so determined and ingrained, a spirit so lost to good and grace, a conscience so seared, and a heart so wilfully hardened that Christ (but only Christ) could declare that such men were lost, 'of their father the Devil and doing his desires.' Like the friar in Dante's Inferno, their souls were in Hell while their bodies still walked the earth.

Some Practical Considerations

It follows that no one need be in anxiety over 'the unpardonable sin,' or in any fear that it has been inadvertently committed. No one who thus fears can possibly so disastrously have erred, for the mark of the determinedly

C

and viciously impenitent is a cynical scorn for all the things of God and Christ, and a shocking insensitivity to the spiritual. Mr. Fearing spoils life, and jettisons the joy and peace of mind which he was meant to enjoy. But he is received at last. No penitent was ever rejected for 'the unpardonable sin,' for its very mark is impenitence.

On the other hand, theologically unverifiable though it is, 'the line unseen that crosses every path' can be psychologically demonstrable. There can come a point in the experience of a man where an invincible hardness can set in and enwrap the mind, making change, self-awareness, consciousness of shortcomings and of sin virtually impossible. Rejected truth is difficult to recapture. To receive enlightenment and to turn away, as some strange verses in the *Epistle to the Hebrews* maintain, is to run the risk of never seeing reality and opportunity with like clarity again. Long before the body fails, or the texture of the brain disintegrates, the mind can be so set and hardened, its responses to the stimuli of life become so stereotyped and habitual, that it is quite impossible to quicken nobler aspirations, to stir to life a salutary desire to be rid of sin, or to awaken a clear and challenging conception of God and immortality.

Or, if in such lives an awareness of evil is stirred, it becomes a terrible introverted concept, which seeks no remedy, and aspires to no forgiveness. Evil is at first an intruder which the host resents, and from whose soiling presence it desires to be free. Then it becomes a tolerated guest. At last it eats up its host. The real redeemable personality vanishes, and the grim invader takes its place. It is like the *rata* vine which loops round a great tree in the New Zealand forest, grows stronger and more powerful until it crushes the life from the tree which gave it first support, and in the end stands in its place.

Consider in illustration the story in the Fourth Gospel. The Pharisees, the same group as those we meet in Capernaum, and this time, in their native habitat, Jerusalem, drag into Christ's presence a woman taken in adultery. 'Here she is, Rabbi, taken in the very act. Now the Law of Moses, of course, not our law, but the great Lawgiver's own solemn enactment, is clear enough. It says that such sinners should be stoned. But we are accustomed to your modifications of Moses' code. We therefore bring her to you. Pray, now, what say you?' He bent down and made marks with His finger in the sand on the flagstones of the Temple court-yard. They continued importunately. 'Say now, what shall we do?' He looked up. 'Let the one without sin among you be the first to throw a stone,' He said. '*The* one,' note. 'Surely in a group so eminent there is one man of complete integrity.' Then, bending down, He began again to write on the ground. The account is so insistent on this writing, that there must have been vital significance in it. What did He write?

Whatever He wrote, those who watched, 'convicted by their conscience began to go out one by one, beginning with the eldest down to the last.' Why the order of pre-cedence? Did He communicate something shocking and convicting, ironically following the order of seniority of which the Pharisees were so fond? Watching His moving finger did the eldest stone-thrower see a name emerging? 'But she is dead, and that was twenty years ago.' He drops his stone and slips away. Another sees a date, a date he has succeeded in banishing from his mind for many a day. He departs. Another reads 'Ephesus? Yes, Ephesus, the Temple of Diana, that woman. But no other Jew saw me, no one knew.' He slinks off. Fancy? Maybe, but some conviction made them go. Christ had a strange faculty for drawing on a knowledge beyond the knowledge of experience when He chose. That was demonstrated by the well of Sychar, and perhaps here.

But note the awful fact. The conviction of sin was not salutary in any of the harsh Pharisaic band. It stirred no desire for salvation or for cleansing. Any one of them could have knelt by the poor, cowed woman, and said: 'Forgive me, fellow-sinner, and let me seek with you the pardon of God.' None did. All their reaction to conviction of sin was desire for concealment, and escape from the presence of the One who had broken through the hollow crust of their pride and self-esteem. Like things of darkness which shrink from the light, and retire for comfort to the murk, the embarrassed Pharisees fled. Salvation would have been found in exposing the soul to the light, until its benediction and its cleansing disinfected the dark corners, and withered the evil there. But evil had taken control. Will and desire were paralysed by it, and none of them found forgiveness.

There was another who found no forgiveness. There is a figure missing in the vivid story. Where was the man who was also 'taken in adultery'? He was never brought to Christ, never confronted with himself. The woman was. Alone with her at last, the Lord looked at the stricken face and saw repentance there, shame, and longing for better things. 'Does no man accuse you?' He asked. 'None, Sir,' she replied. 'Go,' He said, 'and be a sinner no longer.' It is good when our sin leaves us alone with Christ. We can leave that presence, 'a sinner no longer.'

The Pharisees appear again in Chapters Seven and Eight, and then finally, in alliance with the worldly Sadducees, they appear in the last scene, the plot to murder Jesus. Sin is never static. It issues in action. That action is progressive, and does not stop short of ultimate wickedness. The sin of the Pharisees began in self-esteem, in the foolish and petty fancy that they were better than other men. It proceeded to jealousy and resentment against the One who revealed their absurdity and self-righteousness. Resentment, warmed and entertained in the human heart, breeds the poison of hatred. Hatred corrupts the whole personality, and eats away body and brain. Shakespeare knew what he was about when he made Volumnia, the mother of Coriolanus say:

> I would the gods had nothing else to do
> But to confirm my curses. Could I meet 'em
> But once a day, it would uncloy my heart of
> What lies heavy on it.

'You'll sup with me?' says old Menenius in an effort to cool her consuming hatred. Volumnia replies:

> Anger's my meat. I sup upon myself
> And so shall starve with feeding.

Hatred possessed the wounded Pharisees. We saw it in the story from John's Gospel fill, possess, and dominate the whole person. Like Gulliver tied down by the thousand tiny ropes of Lilliput, each day's self-righteousness, each small surrender, each petty resentment entertained and cherished, had added its small contribution until finally the victim was a helpless log. They had committed the sin without pardon, no one single sin of all the noisome multitude, but each a part of a tragic whole. At last impenitence became a fixed and unalterable state. So they blasphemed the Holy Spirit.

Conclusion

And yet the pity of it. The Pharisees at Capernaum, like

those in the Temple Court, were in the presence of God, and went out unsanctified. Whatever He wrote that day on the sandy floor of the precinct, needed only the sweep of His hand to brush it out. There is no permanence in sin, if it is brought into the fire and light of His presence. Omar, the thirteenth-century Persian poet, was lamentably wrong when he wrote:

> The moving finger writes and having writ
> Moves on: nor all your Piety and wit
>   Can lure it back to cancel half a line,
> Nor all your tears blot out a word of it.

The sad words are, in common experience, true. Our writing is like that which the Persian had in mind, the dire words on the plaster of the wall when Belshazzar made a feast to a thousand of his lords. It would be true to life if each reveller that night saw his own fingers crooked round the pen, for we do write our own doom, inscribe our sin on the very texture of the brain, and cut it on the tissues of the body. We mark its record on the tormented mind, on our children's lives, on society at large. . . .

But Christ reverses the evil process. He 'blots out' sins and transgressions. He 'remembers them no more.' For all His omniscience He forgets, cancels, expunges. Metaphor could be multiplied. And Christ within can blessedly re-produce the other process we described. Just as evil can gain a foothold, become established, eat up and absorb the personality, so too can Christ. Timidly received in hesitant faith, He can take over little by little, surrender by surrender, the life of the one who entertains Him, until at length He dominates, controls, and sanctifies. But this is a vital difference. Evil quenches and obliterates the person. Christ permeates, indwells, inspires. In His completeness the believer too is complete, more truly a person, more significantly alive.

It is a process. Some years ago I quoted in a Keswick Bible reading a verse of the American poetess, Edith Lovejoy Pierce. I had just met her in Chicago. I quote here that same verse, and add another:

> O Christ, Thou art within me like a sea,
>   Filling me as a slowly moving tide.
>   No rock, or stone, or sandbar may abide
> Safe from Thy coming and undrowned in Thee.
>
> Thou dost not break me by the might of storm,
>   But with a calm upsurging from the deep,
>   Thou shuttest me in thine eternal keep,
> Where is no ebb, for fullness in Thy norm.

I often saw the tide race in on the vast Manukau Harbour as a boy. It is a huge sheet of water, and miles of sandbanks fill it at low tide. One could stand on the banks, and hear the hiss of the running sheet of water, as the flow came in. And little by little the great sand plains narrowed, became mere slivers of brown, and disappeared. So comes the inflowing Christ, pouring clean benediction over the shallows of the soul, the mind, the rocks, until He fills in beauty.

THE MAN FROM THE TOMBS

Mark 5. 1-10.

THE opening seventeen verses of Chapter Five in Mark's Gospel tell a strange story. It is not certain where Gadara was. Gerasa is sometimes read in the ancient texts, but the busy town of Gerasa seems too far from the lakeside to be the scene of the encounter with the man among the tombs. The story, after all, says little more than that it was territory municipally controlled by Gadara or Gerasa, and further archaeology in the area will one day, no doubt, sort out the difficulty.

Sir George Adam Smith, Palestine's first and greatest geographer, thought he had identified the grim place. There is a steep declivity down to the lake, and such a place is mentioned in the narrative. He pictures the town as it might have been, the pleasant villas on the high slopes with a view up towards Capernaum, the crowded little waterfront, the high-set amphitheatre, from which the assembled Greeks, who thronged the eastern shores of Galilee, could view, not only the drama of the stage, but also the wide prospect of lake and farmland.

While the geographer examined the area, a peasant unearthed a tombstone. It was a memorial to a soldier of Rome's Fourteenth Legion. At the sight of the worn words carved on the stone, the Gospel story came to life. 'Legion' was the name seized upon by the nameless lost soul of the lakeside tombs.

Evening Encounter

It was a dark night when the Lord and His men came ashore. That much is clear from the close of the last chapter. It was not a pleasant time to hear an ear-splitting yell from a homicidal lunatic. And there he was, emerging from the scattered tombs around the limestone rocks, with fragments of the bonds upon his hands by which the terrified townsfolk had sought to bind him.

He was possessed, says the story, by a legion of demons. The allegation is not to be lightly dismissed. There are phenomena of evil not adequately explained by psychologists. The horrors of Voodooism, with the sudden seizure of bystanders by some demonic alien influence, which destroys individuality, changes the voice, imposes patterns of behaviour remote from normal, these manifestations of something unseen are not to be explained away by known processes of the mind's working. They may be paralleled by similar corruptions of the personality in pagan cults, ancient and modern. To dismiss them as 'an extensive complex of compulsive phenomena' is only to say in more and longer words what the Bible says in few.

But suppose the man among the tombs was suffering from recognizable mental illness, how else could the Lord have dealt with him save in the language of His day? Could he have said: 'Man, you suffer from an extensive complex of compulsive phenomena, a psychic dislocation, a schism in your personality, a schizophrenic delusion. . . ?' He met evil where He always meets it, at the place and point of confession, realization, and understanding. There He can heal. When He healed the blind man He knew that there was no virtue in dust mixed with spittle, and daubed on the eyelids. But the poor man thought that there was virtue in the spittle of a saint, and in grace and pity the Lord met him at the point where his spark of faith and hope could be fanned to life.

'My Name is Legion'

The maniac knew that immense and manifold evil gripped and filled his soul. A legion, Rome's unit of six thousand men, had become for him an awful symbol of himself. Perhaps he had run madly from his village a little shrieking boy, when a Roman patrol closed round it to wreak Nazi-like reprisals for the murder of a member of the occupying forces. Perhaps the memory of his parents, dead and stabbed in the dusty street, drove him to consuming hatred, unspeakable acts of vengeance, sin untold.

He had watched with loathing a legion on the march, spear points glittering, helmets shining on the shoulder where they hung, swords swinging, and the long long lines of boots, boots. . . . Kipling makes a soldier of the Boer War speak of the way they drove him mad:

Don't—don't—don't—don't—look at what's in front of you.
(Boots—boots—boots—boots—movin' up an' down again);
Men—men—men—men—men go mad with watchin' 'em,
      An' there's no discharge in the war!

Try—try—try—try—to think of something different—
Oh—my—God—keep—me from goin' lunatic!
(Boots—boots—boots—boots—movin' up an' down again!)
      There's no discharge in the war!

Count—count—count—count—the bullets in the bandoliers.
If—your—eyes—drop—they will get atop o' you!

(Boots—boots—boots—boots—movin' up an' down again)
    There's no discharge in the war.

'Taint—so—bad—by—day because o' company,
But night—brings—long—strings—o' forty thousand million
Boots—boots—boots—boots—movin' up an' down again
    There's no discharge in the war![1]

Legion! Perhaps it was like that, day and night, the tramp, tramp, tramp, tramp of marching hosts of vicious things. Occupying cohorts of foul presences held the mind and heart in cruel subjection. And there among the tombs he saw the memorials of them, Legion, Legion, Legion, cut in stone until he shrieked, and tore things apart. What had they to do with Christ, such a regiment of horror? Everything. Some undamaged corner of the will cried out for salvation. But how could Christ convince so shattered a soul that it was healed, cleansed and free? It costs much sometimes to effect such salvation. The price is not always mentioned. It is, in this story. It cost two thousand swine. Hands are raised in horror at such a sacrifice. Vegetarians only have some shadow of right to such protest, for my butcher assures me that two thousand pigs would not keep New Zealand in bacon and pork for one day. The sacrifice of Gadara is repeated daily in one small land, not to restore a soul and bestow the blessed gift of peace, but to provide the Englishman's breakfast, or a crackly joint for dinner. There were three gates to the nether world, said the Rabbis. One was in the desert, one in the sea, a third was at Jerusalem. The man would know that the evil was gone where it belonged.

  [1] From *The Five Nations*, by permission of Mrs. George Bambridge, Methuen & Co. Ltd., the Macmillan Co. of Canada and Doubleday & Co. Inc.

Peace of Mind

Peace and sanity are beyond all price. A quiet conscience, freedom from fear, tranquillity must be pursued at any price. Position, pleasure, money, popularity, success are worthless baubles without them. 'What is your name?' asked the Lord. 'There are so many of me,' moaned the man, 'that I am a whole host of people; so I call myself Legion.' The edge of that experience, is known to all of us. 'Dear Lord, that loose, lascivious face,' cried Studdart Kennedy, 'that leers in my own soul, wilt Thou not smash it with Thy cross, and make me free and whole?' Paul spoke of 'the other law in our members, warring against the law of our minds', the unwanted presence which makes us 'do what we would not.'

A legion of impulses, appetites, temptations, conventions invade us, corrupt us, and bring us down to death. They obliterate the personality, oppress the true self, until we are lost to God and joy. And 'some such grievous passions tear,' that only Christ can cast them out.

From the man of Gadara, Christ cast them out. The poor creature fell silent, his convulsive movements ceased. Calm poured through him like a blessed, cleansing stream. A kindly member of the band tossed him his fisherman's cloak, and when the people of the town arrived, the man was sitting clothed and in his right mind. It was a sight to call for benedictions on the Visitor. They, too, needed His healing touch, but they had not recognized their sickness. There are souls not awed by the vision of beauty and goodness. Sunset and evening star mean nothing to them. In Christ they 'see no beauty that they should desire Him.' Harold St. John's original commentary on Mark reminds us of John Oxenham's poem. They beg Christ to be gone:

Rabbi, begone!
> Thy powers bring loss to us and ours!
>> Our ways are not as Thine—
>>> Thou lovest men—we, swine!

O get Thee gone, Omnipotence
> And take this fool of Thine!
>> His soul? What care we for his soul,
>>> Since we have lost our swine?

The Christ went sadly,
> He had wrought for them a sign
>> Of love and tenderness divine—
>>> They wanted swine!

Christ stands without your door and gently knocks,
> But if your gold or swine the entrance blocks,
>> He forces no man's hold, He will depart
>>> And leave you to the treasures of your heart.

It was a strange sight on the beach. The glorious revelation of God's power to save a soul was before them. They gave no heed. He stepped into the boat. The younger men thrust hard at the gunwale. The ship floated. The oars began to dip. They could still have called him back. They preferred swine.

The Inconvenient Guest

The Gadarenes are still with us. They are not always hostile to Christianity, but it must not upset their way of life. Christ may land on the shore of their lives with all He has to give, but He must cost them nothing, He must cause no disruption of their manner of living, He must occasion no discomfort.

On such terms He is unable to stay. He can be an inconvenient guest, if he encounters selfishness, carnality, and materialism enthroned in the house. He can upset old friendships, for 'what fellowship has Christ and Belial?' He can divide families. He warned as much. 'I bring not peace but a sword,' He said. He devastates preoccupation with gain and with material things. He met a moral young man thus preoccupied. In one sentence He exposed the limits of his sincerity and the shallowness of his desire. 'Go,' He said, 'sell what you have and give it to the poor, and come and follow me.' He ruins careers. He destroyed that of Matthew and Zacchaeus. He brings ostracism. 'They will persecute you for my name's sake,' He warned.

But in return He brings new and deeper friendships; He unites in a larger family; He provides treasures in Heaven; He gives new and nobler careers. In a word He fulfils His promise to give 'life more abundantly.'

First Missionary to the Greeks

The folk of Gadara have left the stage, faceless and unblessed. They returned to 'the husks the swine did eat.' Opportunity had come and gone. 'The harvest is passed and the summer is ended,' runs the saddest verse in Jeremiah, 'and we are not saved.' The harvest on the Gadarene beach was one soul redeemed, one tormented mind healed.

It must have been bright morning by this time. As the party climbed back into the boat, the man from the tombs begged to join the party. The Lord refused and sent him back to the community which had ostracized and scorned and feared him. 'And he departed,' runs the story, 'and began to publish in Decapolis how great things Jesus had done for him: and all men did marvel.' Or read it in Edward Vernon's interesting paraphrase: ' "No," Jesus said to him, "you must go home—back to your own people, and tell them what God has done for you, and how he took pity on you." The man turned away and went off; and all over Ten-Town-Land he spread the story of what Jesus had done for him. What a sensation it caused.'

The Decapolis, or 'Ten-Town-Land,' lay east of the Sea of Galilee. It was cosmopolitan and swarmed with Greeks. Gadara was one of the ten towns which gave the region its name. Damascus was the largest and most northerly. It is difficult at this distance in time to estimate what the population may have been, but a million people may have lived in the Decapolis, predominantly Gentile. Immigrant Greeks gave form and flavour to the busy life of the region. In Gerasa, modern Jarash, of which extensive ruins remain, Roman and Italian mingled with Greek. The columned oval of the market-place still stands, and one can picture it swarming with traders, camel-men in town with loaded beasts from Syria and the Euphrates Valley, or from the complex of caravan routes which struck north-east through waste and mountain to connect with the long roads of inland Asia. To one of the towns of the Decapolis the Prodigal Son came, if the story is from life, with money in his pocket, and ripe for the fleecing which awaited the unsophisticated in the cosmopolitan towns.

Into this varied throng came the first Christian missionary to be mentioned in the Bible, the first 'apostle to the Gentiles,' for the mission of the Twelve had been to Israel and Galilee. He is the first to be mentioned in the New Testament as one sent 'into all the world to preach the Gospel.' In the Decapolis, as nowhere else, the outer world pressed on Palestine. He was told to stay in his own place, the hardest place of all in which to witness. The man from the lakeside graveyard was shown the truth, which the Christian

Church has too often forgotten, that the mission-field begins in front of the feet of every follower of Christ. He was the first to illustrate in his person and commission the pattern which should be borne steadfastly in mind—the widening circles of our obligation and our witness, 'in Jerusalem, in all Judaea, in Samaria, and unto the uttermost parts of the earth.'

Pilgrim's Progress

After the rich fashion of all that Christ did, the story is crowded with lessons. It was natural enough that the healed man should desire to remain near the One who had healed him—but the danger was, with one so healed, that the whole story would end there. It was vital to turn his lonely gaze outward, and restore him to the society from which he had fled. The Lord, said John, 'knew what was in man,' and He treats us all according to our needs. Mary, too involved with life, with a wild and carnal past in the mad whirl of the city's night life, chose the better part when she sat still, and learned rest and quietness at Jesus' feet.

Not so the solitary. Cardinal Newman once remarked: 'The medieval monk proposed to himself no great or systematic work, beyond that of saving his own soul; his vocation was a flight from the world and nothing else.' There is no health or usefulness in such withdrawal if it becomes a pattern of life. The *Pilgrim's Progress*, with its flight from the City of Destruction, tells only half the story. That is why C. S. Lewis's phantasy, the *Pilgrim's Regress*, sends the redeemed man back along the path which he had travelled. We should seek to do the same. Times of fellowship, withdrawal and retreat are essential for the soul's well-being, but they should be followed by return.

Toynbee, the great historian, has shown that a pattern of history is involved. In the lives of men and of nations, there is a consistent phenomenon of Withdrawal and Return. Israel in Egypt, Judah in Babylon, Moses in Midian, David in Engedi, Paul in Arabia, are Biblical illustrations. You who read are another. The Ten Towns await you. Choose any you will. Between us we could cover our native land. There is need there, and to them you can carry the one who supplies man's need, the living Christ.

Indeed, only in your person does He walk 'England's green and pleasant land.' 'All men marvelled,' Mark concludes, and it was a cause for wonder that the scorned and rejected should not repudiate the society which had caused him pain, or return only with a gospel of searing hate, determined to pull down that which had hurt him. He had known and suffered the strength of hate. It was no motive force for the service he now sought. The theme was 'how great things God had done for him,' and God plants no hate, no bitterness or scorn in any heart.

'All men marvelled,' that Christ could depart and yet manifestly remain behind and walk among them. Christ moves among the Ten Towns still in the lives of those who bear Him witness. His love; His power to save; His courtesy; His grace; His strength and quiet courage are seen in the persons of those who serve Him. And at times we carry His cross.

That, perhaps, was the thought for which the imagination of those who invented the story of *Quo Vadis?* was feeling. Where the Appian Way still runs into Rome it is possible to imagine the centuries away. It is an ancient landscape as one comes in from the Catecomb of St. Callixtus, and if the point of view is chosen, and modern buildings excluded, one might imagine that it is A.D. 64 with

D

Nero's persecution raging. It is here, by the bus terminal, that the Church of Quo Vadis marks the spot of the legend.

Peter was escaping from Rome. Here outside the walks, runs the tale, he met Christ, '*Quo vadis, Domine?*' he said. 'Where are you going, Lord?' 'To Rome', the Lord replied, 'to be crucified again.' Peter returned, says the legend, and suffered martyrdom. Of course Christ could not be literally crucified afresh. That can be done only in the souls of those who reject Him. Calvary was once for all. But there is a sense in which those who follow Christ reproduce Him in their lives. Peter and Paul both speak of a fellowship of suffering between the believer and his Lord. There is also a fellowship of joy, of peace, of love. In very truth Christ stayed in the Ten Towns. So can we. But why should I fumble for words when it has already been said so penetratingly in the New Testament. Do you remember the passage of Christ's descent to the cross and ascent to glory in the Second Chapter of the Epistle to the Philippians? I have translated seven verses to form my appeal to you:

Have this mind in you, the mind which was in Christ Jesus, who, though he was once in the likeness of God, did not consider equality with God something to be usurped, but emptied Himself, and took on the likeness of a slave. And, in human shape, He humbled Himself, becoming obedient to death, even the death of the cross. Wherefore God has greatly exalted Him, and has granted Him as a gift the Name that is above every name, so that in the Name of Jesus every knee should bow in all imaginable realms, and every tongue should confess that Jesus Christ is Lord, that God may be glorified.

PARTY AT MACHAERUS

Mark 6. 14-29.

THE mission of the Twelve through the villages of Galilee stirred the guilty conscience of Herod Antipas, the tetrarch of the land, the contemptible son of Herod the Elder, the scoundrel of the Nativity story. 'It is John the Baptist,' whispered the ruler, when he heard of Christ. 'John the Baptist whom I beheaded risen from the dead.' And Mark adds a curious detail: 'For Herod feared John, knowing that he was a just man and an holy, and he observed him; and when he heard him he did many things and heard him gladly.' Or to paraphrase in simple English: 'Herod respected John. He knew that he was a just, good man, and paid attention to him. He listened willingly to John's preaching, and John's words deeply influenced his conduct.'

It is a strangely moving picture of what might have been. The New Testament has little good to say of the five Herods who move through its pages, and to Herod Antipas the Lord had no word to say. 'That fox,' He called him in one rare phrase of scorn. And yet here is the memory of a brighter hour, with desire for good, and admiration for a good man, still alive and active in a life which became utterly corrupt. Here too is conscience moving, and the sharp sting of remembered sin. Here is the puppet prince of Galilee with the disguises torn away and the defences stripped, a frightened man tormented by a memory, alone with himself and God.

The Recognition

When the clever Greek, Aristotle, analysed the tragic drama of his land's great literature, he pointed out that a fearful moment comes in tragedy which he called the Recognition. It is a moment of crisis and revelation, when some mad, blind, or corrupted spirit sees at last the awfu truth which has evaded understanding until that point o time. Too late the realization breaks of what is, and wha might have been, of a present built of folly and falsehood of a past beyond recall. The tensest scenes on the tragic stage contain these moments of truth. 'Now I know, then ought I to have known?' cried Euripides' Jason. Tearing out his eyes, Sophocles' Oedipus sees that he, *he* is the corruption he had sought in Thebes, Macbeth meets dispair, Lear and Othello recognize their folly. . . .

Antipas meets such a moment in Mark's simple and revealing story. It is the Recognition . . . that crime cannot quench a guilty fear, that evil cannot be ended where the evil-doer desires it to be ended, that self can be a grim companion. Was it not President Coolidge who said: 'I must think well of myself; I live with myself; I eat with myself; I sleep with myself; and one day I must die with myself. It is essential that I think well of myself.'

The Conscience

Conscience, Herod's tormentor, was once his friend. Conscience can be the point of God's Spirit's impact on the soul, the bridgehead for His blessed invasion. Relentlessly, God pursues the soul of man, presses hard upon his sin, and stirs divine restlessness which can find its peace only in surrender. That strange, lush poem of Francis Thompson, built of his own delinquency, captures the thought in its violent imagery:

I fled him down the nights and down the days,
I fled him down the arches of the years;
I fled Him down the labyrinthine ways
Of my own mind, and in the mist of tears
I hid from Him, and under running laughter.
 Up vistaed hopes I sped;
 And shot, precipitated,
Adown Titanic glooms of chasm'd fears
From those strong Feet which followed, followed after.

A man is truly lost when God ceases to pursue him. Christ followed Judas to the brink of his last passionate refusal. He washed the traitor's feet with the rest, and it was only after that final act of appeal that He looked at him, and said in flat, chill tones: 'That which you do, do quickly.' And Judas, says John, went out. He adds three symbolic words, which form one of the most awful phrases in the Bible: 'It was night.'

There was a point, too, at which Herod likewise stepped into the dark. Perhaps it may be located in the story told by Mark of the birthday party at Machaerus. It is ironical that a birthday should be a day of death, but so it was. Like the Greek tragedy already used for illustration, the actors in this drama move on a remote, exalted stage, set apart a little that the audience may see and review them. The motives, springs of action, the fears, the follies, the sin, and tragic outcome, are not remote or in any way withdrawn. That is why the story of the Machaerus feast is worth a second look. It is re-enacted a thousand times a day.

The Story

It must have been somewhere before A.D. 23 that Herod Antipas met Herodias, his brother Philip's wife. This Philip was not his fellow-ruler, but another member of the numerous Herod family, who lived quietly in Rome, and abjured the stormy politics of Palestine. Herodias, also a relative, took less kindly to a life of ease and obscurity, and when the more dynamic brother, Herod Antipas, appeared in Rome, she set herself to win him. It was not difficult. Such women bend the carnal, the sensual, and the weak where they will. Herod knew the brief sense of victory, achievement, and exhilaration sensed by fools when they think they have won cheap pleasure without a price in pain and shame. Such bills are presented later.

Herodias was of royal blood, and sought no humiliating liaison. She must be Herod's queen. The weakling promised, and the twain set out for Palestine. Herod's rightful queen soon heard the truth from her spies, or Herod's many foes. She was the fiery daughter of the King of the Nabataeans, the Arab tribe whose capital was the rock-cut city of Petra, and she was not one to receive such vicious insults lightly. She fled to her father, and her father raised the desert tribes, and marched on Palestine.

It was a stormy frontier, and part of the duty of the puppet kings of Palestine was to police the march-lands and not provoke petty wars like this. Hence the task which awaited Herod, as soon as he returned to Palestine. He moved his armed forces to the great stronghold of Machaerus, one of the fortresses by which his father had sought to bolster the desert defences of the land. It was not safe to leave Herodias in the royal city of Tiberias. Hence her presence with the officers and staff on Herod's birthday.

And in the dungeon beneath lay John the Baptist, who had greeted the royal crime with fearless denunciation, describing in plain, frank terms the vicious licence of the deed, and shaming the culprits before the land. Perhaps the preacher's words had some effect on Herod. Perhaps it was

a moment he might have seized, a chance of salvation.
Some deep apprehension accounts for the implacable
hatred of the woman. Having won so much, she did not
intend to weaken now.

The Feast

There is no doubt that Herodias's wicked mind contrived
the whole situation. She knew the man she had trapped.
She knew the devices by which she had trapped him. She
knew the open door into his mind. Hence the base use to
which she put her daughter Salome. The girl was probably
sixteen or seventeen years of age, with the warm beauty of
all the Herodian women. She had accompanied her mother
on her flight to Palestine, and was now to be her mother's
effective tool. Herodias touched darker depths at this
moment than she had touched before. She had corrupted a
man. She was to use her daughter to corrupt him further.

John had reminded Herodias of the Law, which stood in
the path of her inordinate ambition. She wanted nothing to
remind her of that Law, or perhaps rather nothing to remind her less determined partner in sin of the Law. But
neither God nor God's law can be permanently avoided by
putting aside that which reminds of both. Somewhere, at
some time, the Law must be confronted, somewhere God
is met face to face. All Herodias's schemes came to nought.
She and her victim failed, and met ignominy and exile.

At the Machaerus feast all seemed so near success. One
more crime to complete and cover up the last, and all
would assuredly be well. That is ancient folly, as another
king of Palestine had found when he walked on the palace
roof in the evening, and fell a victim to a clever woman,
and murdered the woman's husband when the sin called for

covering. Sin leads to sin. It cannot be confined or isolated. The thing is insatiable, until it ruins the soul.

Herod was ruined that night. Picture the scene. Herodias has it all arranged with Salome. The girl glides in demanding all eyes. Conversation, the loud laughter of the half-drunken throng dies down. Whirling, writhing, the slim young girl dances some voluptuous Arabian dance, casting aside veils and robes to some bold, base climax of carnality. Fired, half-maddened by the spectacle, which Herodias, knowing him, had arranged so well, Herod made his mad promise. Let her ask. Anything. It should be hers. Herodias dictated the answer: 'The head of John the Baptist.' The trap closed on cowardice and vice.

Herod's Moment

But the moment of Herod's damnation was not yet. He could have still retreated. He was trapped, and knew that he was trapped, and yet 'for his oath's sake, and for their sake who sat at meat with him, he would not reject her.' There are oaths better broken, promises better not kept, partnerships better dissolved, undertakings better repudiated. So, too, there are observers better scorned, laughter better disregarded, criticism better treated with contempt, censure which it is honour to incur. 'For their sake who sat at meat with him. . . .' Who were they? If any among them would say: 'Herod promised, but drew back when the promise called for crime. Herod therefore sinned . . .' if any could thus confuse all morality and confound all law, they were as ripe for ruin as the king who hesitated, as damned as the woman who organized the base dilemma.

Herod could still have been saved, even after the flesh had betrayed him, even after sensuality had brought him to the bottom rung of moral disaster. The way back goes far down the slope. The grace of God reaches infinitely far. Herod had only to treat with scorn the laughter of vicious men. He had only one small step of right to take, and it might have saved his feet from last catastrophe. He failed to take it, and when he at last met Christ, Christ Himself had no point of contact, no single word which he might have grasped and understood. Here was Hell indeed. Hell self-made and self-created. Herod had lived in it since his birthday at Machaerus.

The Recognition Again

There is a Recognition of another sort. There are times of opportunity, moments of possibility, when God speaks, when the issues of life stand out sharp and clear, when sin and salvation assume simplicity and significance, and comprehend the whole of life. There are hours of lucidity, when it seems possible, in God's strength, to break some evil chain of cause and effect, and in new strength make a sanctified fresh beginning.

Treat such moments well, for they partake of eternity. Treated with contempt, they pass, become less lucid and compelling, more rare in experience. Every act is a cause an effect. Events do not stand in isolation. Act begets act. Sin produces sin. You cannot, in any wrong, 'trammel up the consequences.' So mused Macbeth, and he was touching truth, or Shakespeare was in his inimitable way:

> If it were done when 'tis done, then 'twere well
> It were done quickly; if the assassination
> Could trammel up the consequence, and catch
> With his surcease success; that but this blow
> Might be the be-all and the end-all here,
> And here, upon this bank and shoal of time
> We'd jump the life to come.

No sin is done when it is done. It breaks open a new flowing source of evil. No wrong act is the be-all and the end-all. Nor can it be confined to 'this bank and shoal of time'. There is still 'the life to come'. Salome slipped into Herod's life with Herodias the night they hurried out of Rome to take ship at Ostia on the Tiber's mouth. She came for ever.

Herod's Dilemma

But turn back to the text. It has been quoted above in the form in which it appears in the Authorized Version. That version, in one word, follows a text which is not the best attested. Another reading with the change of only one vital letter, would give a rendering: 'he was perplexed in many ways,' for 'he did many things.' Hence the translation in the New English Bible: 'He liked to listen to him though the listening left him greatly perplexed.' The 'observed' of the Authorized Version is also not the most lucid rendering.

Let us go back to the Greek text, and try again. Here is my translation: 'Herod revered John, knowing him to be a just and saintly man, and he kept him by him, and when he heard him was very perplexed, and yet he was glad to listen to him.' It was a curious dilemma, but a common one. Why was Herod perplexed? Because of a divided mind. He saw the right, but knew what it would cost. He saw with more clarity than some that he could not live in both camps, serve two masters, hold fast to his sin, but win salvation. He was perplexed because he could see no logical adjustment to his mode of life which would leave him the enjoyment of the vices he loved, and yet remove the load from his conscience.

His folly lay in the over-estimate of the worth of the

trash he hesitated to abandon. No real or abiding pleasure is diminished by surrender to God. All else that matters or endures is given in Him. It is in the service of evil that things coveted are costly, and sham into the bad bargain. As Lowell puts it:

> At the Devil's booth are all things sold,
> Each ounce of dross costs its pound of gold,
> For a cap and bells our lives we pay,
> Bubbles we buy with a whole soul's tasking.
> 'Tis only God that is given away,
> Heaven alone may be had for the asking.

Herod, along with multitudes, found it difficult to see this simple truth.

What should a man do who feels the tug of God upon his conscience, who hears what his heart tells him is true? He should at all costs obey. Obeying will bring enlightenment and a true apprehension of the cost. He who madly promised half his kingdom as the price of a sensual thrill, would have sacrificed none of his kingdom for obedience to God. He could have held his royalty, enriched and secure. So too in lives less exalted. The realization of the truth comes with action. It is the other sort of Recognition of which we spoke.

Read H. G. Well's *Kingdom of the Blind*. A mountaineer in the Andes, caught in a glissade, slid down into a deep, dark valley. His life was miraculously preserved by a sudden snowdrift, and alive but imprisoned he struggled down through the pines and found a strange village. It was neat and ordered, with kerbed geometrical paths. The houses were daubed with multicoloured paint, and in the hot morning sun everyone was asleep.

Then he remembered a half-forgotten story. Cut off by

great landslides, a community of mountain folk had been lost to the world. Some mysterious condition of the air had robbed them all of sight. Their children were born blind, and the eyes of all withered. That was centuries ago, and the world had forgotten.

Now he had found it. It was the Land of the Blind, and there, reflected the newcomer, the man with sight would be king. How wrong he was. The blind community proved more than a match for him. Long lost to the common world, they had built a mythology of their own. All words for sight and colour had long been lost from their vocabulary. They worked in the cool time, which was night. They slept in the warm time. They believed in winged angels. They heard their flight and also their songs at dawn. Above, a shining ceiling of smooth rock closed their abode. In vain the visitor spoke to them of dawn and sunset, and the solemn beauty of the sky, and the snow on the mighty peaks. They thought him mad, and the wise men among them diagnosed as his malady the effect of the fluttering globes upon his face.

Gradually the atmosphere entangled him. Little by little, the narrow world he had found became his own. At last, for love of a girl, he agreed to be like them. They should remove his eyes, make him the same as they were, and absorb him into their blind community.

On the morning of the day when the operation was to take place, the mountaineer went out to look for the last time on the beauty of the pink dawn on the uplifted snows. His practised eye surveyed a slope. Up there through the pines, across that steep scree, up the funnel through the snow, the saddle, and the peak. . . . One might make it. All his being cried out for escape. He began to climb.

He climbed all day, and when the sun sank he was safe on

the ridge. The valley beneath was a gloom of purple darkness and the last rays of the sun turned the tiny mountain
flowers in the rocks into things of exquisite beauty.

When God speaks and bids you escape from the valley of
the blind, climb. When the heart responds with longing for
higher things, climb. When the free spirit revolts against a
mad society, break away and climb. . . .

ON THE MOUNTAIN AND AFTER

Mark 9. 2-29.

THE major portion of Mark's Gospel lies behind us as we turn to Chapter Nine. In Chapter Eight, in fact, we pass to the final tremendous scenes of the Lord's ministry. He no longer addresses the multitudes, calling the nation to repentance. He speaks only to small groups and individuals. Above all He seeks to prepare His own men for the ordeal which lies ahead.

The scene is Caesarea Philippi, Philip's Caesarea, in other words, to distinguish it from Herod's Caesarea on the Mediterranean coast. It was a lovely region. There on the lower slopes of Hermon the Jordan had its source from two clear springs. The first Greek immigrants had built a shrine to their god Pan there, and called the place Paneas. It is Baniyas to this day. Philip, the tetrarch, had adorned the place and renamed it in honour of Caesar and himself. It was here that the Lord sought retreat.

He had much to say to His men, and it was somewhere in this pleasant countryside that Peter gladdened his Master's heart by the insight of his great confession. Here it was also that the same Peter earned His stern rebuke by the horror with which he received the Lord's stark, clear announcement of His coming suffering and death. It was a week later when the same Peter was granted the Vision Splendid.

There is no doubt that the Transfiguration took place on Hermon, or one of its lower foothills. The peak lifted its snowy summit fourteen miles north of Caesarea Philippi.

Tabor, which Jerome named as the Mount of the Trans-figuration, was fifty miles away in the south of Galilee. Tabor's low top was also occupied by a fort called Itaby-rium. It was no place for the scene of heavenly mystery. On Hermon was the clean loneliness which the Lord sought.

The Purpose of the Vision

The Valley of the Shadow lay ahead. Peter, James and John were to be the leaders in that dark ravine, and the Lord sought in a special way to fortify their soul for the ordeal. In both of Peter's epistles, written a generation later, there is reference to the awesome experience. Mark, too, has some homely features in his account which catch the very sound of Peter's voice as he detailed the tremen-dous story. The expression, 'exceeding white, so as no laundryman on earth could whiten them,' is in Mark alone. Mark bluntly reports that Peter's suggestion about the three tents were made by a man 'not knowing what he said.' It was always Peter's way to hide tension or embar-rassment by saying something, anything which sprang to his mind. It was a frequent source of folly.

Testing and temptation were to take two forms in the coming weeks of trial and misery. First they were to be tempted to think that they had been wrong about Christ. John, alone in the dungeons of Machaerus, had doubted thus. One of those who walked to Emmaus said wistfully: 'We trusted that it had been He who should redeem Israel.' To strengthen three men against this moment, the Lord revealed Himself as the consummation of all Israel's history.

For minds steeped in that ancient story there was over-whelming significance in the appearance of Moses and Elijah. Those trained to see the analogies and parallelisms of the Old Testament would remember that both Moses and

Elijah died strange deaths, both east of Jordan, that two mountains, Horeb and Nebo, were in the story of one, two mountains, Horeb and Carmel, in the life of the other. The cloud that misted Hermon would recall the clouds of Sinai into which Moses went, and the cloud which came up out of the sea after Elijah's victory. Moses was the leader of the Exodus, and in the Greek text of Luke's account we read that the twain spoke with Christ of the 'exodus' He should accomplish at Jerusalem. Elijah, like Christ, knew an Ascension. Moses was the great Law-giver, Elijah the first of the prophets. All the Old Testament was embodied in them. Words, too, would echo in the minds of the three, old oracles chanted in the Sunagogue, and heard on the rabbis' lips a thousand times. Verses from Deuteronomy (18, 15–19), words uttered to Moses, would spring into the memory: 'I will raise up a Prophet from among their brethren like unto thee, and will put my words in his mouth. . . .' And from the last of the Old Testament writers, Malachi (3. 1; 4. 5, 6): 'Behold I will send you Elijah, the prophet, before the great and dreadful day of the Lord. . . .'

Those who shared the solemn hour on Hermon could never, in their most harassed moments doubt that their Master was 'the One Who Should Come'. Herein lies often the purpose of some deep spiritual experience. God who knows what is to be, and the trial it is in his vast purpose to permit, braces and steadies the soul that His servant may be able to bear it. Nor, as Principal Edman of Wheaton once wrote in the flyleaf of a book which he gave me, should we ever doubt in the dark what God told us in the light.

God in the Shadows

The second form of their coming testing was the tempta-

tion to despair, and to imagine that God had lost control
and that evil was triumphant. In that temptation lies the
darkest hour of the soul. That is why Christ, so soon to
hang broken and bleeding on the cross, is revealed as
'the Beloved Son.' And we are 'accepted in the Beloved,'
as the thrilling verse in Ephesians puts it.

This is our steadying thought, when evil seems hideously
strong, and wrong triumphant, with 'Truth forever on the
scaffold, Wrong forever on the throne.' It is well at such
times to remember the next line which rhymes with the
line I quoted: 'Standeth God within the shadow, keeping
watch above His own.' If that is not true, I have no good
news to preach, no gospel, no purpose in writing thus, and
'they have taken away my Lord, and I know not where
they have laid Him.' If suffering is aimless, if we cannot
bring our panic fears to God, and expect Him to hear our
prayer, and bend in a Father's mercy, if endurance is the
one quality for which we can rightly pray, then I do not
understand Jesus Christ. I do not know what the Lord's
Prayer means, and I am 'of all men most miserable.'

'I had fainted,' thus runs the Thirteenth Verse of Psalm
Twenty-Seven, 'unless I had believed to see the goodness of
the Lord in the land of the living.' The main clause is
italicized. Lamentably the translators inserted it. All the
Hebrew says in that slow, wondering sentence is: '. . . unless I had believed to see the goodness of the Lord in the
land of the living!' Supply the rest from experience: 'I had
fallen, I had despaired, I had lost all faith, poise, hope, joy,
I had cast all religion to the wild winds . . . unless I had believed that here, not in a bright hereafter, but here, in the
murk and turmoil of a corrupted world, here in the stum-
bling flesh, I can gain knowledge of a good and loving God,
One who cares, keeps, heals the spirit, restores the soul. . . . I

E

had sealed my lips, abandoned preaching, fallen cynical and silent, with nought to say, nothing to which to cling, had I not believed in a Hand that guides, a Heart that plans, a Love which will not let me go. . . .'

Shattering days lay ahead. Three men were granted the vision of a truth above all lies, deceptions, shams, betrayals. Time was to pass before they sensed its full reality. Peter's blundering words show how small was their understanding. He was a man of action, but also a man of words, too prone to blurt out the unformed utterance of the moment. He called for three tents in manifold error. He was ranking his Lord with Moses and Elijah, in spite of the noble confession a week before. He was snatching, too, at the old rallying-cry of Israel: 'To your tents', in the wild surmise that the Hour had come, and all the rebel nation needed was a banner and a havoc-cry. It is the sorry manner of man to misunderstand God's finest gifts. Or was Peter seeking to prolong the hour of vital experience, to hold the Eternal to an hour of time, and pin the Almighty to a place?

In the quietness of our own mind Christ can be transfigured. As He invested the fallen snow, the white mists of Hermon, His woven garment, with the bright glory of God, so here He can transform our common lives, and make all experiences more meaningful in the glow of His nearer presence. We do well to look and listen and fix the scene on heart and mind, for we know not what next week holds.

Descent from the Mountain

I well remember a contrast of a few years ago. I had spent a week at the Keswick Convention—a golden week of sunshine in that incomparable summer of 1959. The days were rich in fellowship, and it seemed a good and quiet world in the little grey town thronged with Christian men and women. . . . A week later we were driving south. The green of Lakeland darkens into the industrial wilderness of Westmorland and Lancashire. We threaded town on town, sooty streets crowded with England's multitude. Slum fused with slum. A grimy chapel displayed a pathetic notice in its deserted forecourt: 'Won't you help the Church?' it ran. The faceless multitude crowding the grim streets, the heavy atmosphere of boredom and discontent, made us feel alien, lonely, and disturbed. It needed only a winter twilight drizzle to complete C. S. Lewis's picture of Hell. . . . We saw it all from the car window, and saw it, no doubt, one-sidedly. In the mean streets and packed tenements was surely some human kindness, Christian grace, and sacrificial service. Darkest England must have its gleams of light. But after Keswick it was like the foot of the mountain, the chilling contact with another side of life. The supernatural shekinah was gone. It was the muted light of common day.

So it was when the three men came down from the mountain with their Master, charged, in the meantime, to tell no one what they had seen. A considerable crowd awaited them, 'a great multitude', Mark says, with some intermingling of doctors-of-the-law from Caesarea Philippi. It is difficult to account for such a popular demonstration unless some unwise boasting or courting of popularity on the part of the disciples is the reason for it. We shall return to that thought.

The centre of interest was a stricken man, in agony of mind over his son. He had come to seek Christ's help for the afflicted lad, who was torn and tormented by an Evil Thing which possessed him. There is no greater pain than the helpless anguish of a parent who would gladly bear the burden of a child's woe, but can only watch and grieve. 'Absalom, my son, my son, would I had died for thee.' 'Sir, come down ere my child die.' Such cries of the heart ring down the centuries with no loss of sharp and urgent reality. Let it be said that such experience is shared by God. It is part of the mystery of divine love that God so yearns over sinners. God's love is no remote and incomprehensible emotion unfathomable though its depths must be. If 'the Only Begotten Son revealed Him' in truth, and translated into comprehensible language the Person of God Himself, God's love is the love of Jesus Christ. On the crest of Olivet, He wept over Jerusalem and cried: 'O Jerusalem, Jerusalem, thou that killest the prophets, and stonest those who are sent unto thee, how often would I have gathered your children together even as a hen gathers her chickens under her wing, but ye would not.' We dare not think of the love of God in other terms, and this love is the recognizable love of a parent for an afflicted, rebellious, or wayward child.

Let that thought, therefore, be for comfort in such an hour. Men and women, as Rupert Brooke put it, can be 'washed gloriously with sorrow', and in the experience of pain God may be found. But let this also be said: Let sons and daughters beware how they thoughtlessly inflict such grief. Let them not treat lightly or contemptuously a parent's love.

The Church in the Way

The man who came seeking Christ found the Church. Christ's followers stood between the Lord and the man who sought His aid. We read in Chapter Two how the four eager friends who brought the palsied man to Christ 'could not come nigh to Him because of the press'. Perhaps it was Peter who sent the men down to his boat for an armful of rope, and helped them to lower the sick man through the broken roof. It sometimes requires uncommon inventiveness to get through the screen of humanity, and find the Lord. Down at Jericho blind Bartimaeus shouted his way through the obstructing crowds.

It is tragic when the multitude in the path are Christ's professed followers. Godless doctrines of exclusiveness seek sometimes deliberately to clutter the path. Barriers of inquisition and regulation fence the way. Men intrude with tests and shibboleths. Worst of all, crass, insensitive sin denies the hungry the food they seek, the seeker his vision of the Lord. I shall never forget a letter I once read in a London newspaper in 1924. I forget the nature of the controversy which provoked it, but the tale it told has gone with me for forty years. Perhaps I remember it so well because I was just back from a visit to the battlefields of the Somme. I had wandered round Thiepval, Bray, Flers, and Delville Wood, names of horror to a generation. It was still as the conflict had left it, a broken, shell-torn countryside, tangled with rusting wire.

Back in London I read the letter in the newspaper. Someone described how his regiment had landed in Dover, coming home on leave. It was Sunday morning, and the men were anxious, for the faint ominous sound of big guns was on the southern breeze. Then came the shocking news. Leave was cancelled and they were to return. The first battle of the Somme had commenced. Waiting for the ship to clear, ready for re-embarkation, the men were marched to church. They sat in khaki lines, so soon to be in the wake of the barrage again and the bullet-swept brown valley. A young man mounted the pulpit, and discussed the purpose of the Epistle to the Ephesians. 'And so, my friends,' he concluded, 'it is evident that the letter was not, in fact addressed to the Ephesian church, but rather to the congregation at Laodicea.'

Men came in cold fear and grief to find Christ. The Church, in the shape of a preacher without convictions, stood in the way. Such folly still blocks the path. If a man cannot point those who seek truth, forgiveness and comfort, to a Lord who can richly provide all three, let him get out of the pulpit. When Alexander the Great visited Diogenes the philosopher in his poor shelter, he asked whether there was any royal boon he could bestow: 'Yes,' said Diogenes, 'you are blocking the sunshine. Stand out of the way.' So let all who diminish Christ, darken counsel, make God remote, too little, the servant of a sect, the patron of a tiny élite, the champion of private dogma, get out of the way. Nor let those crowd round the living Christ whose contaminated lives demonstrate no features of their Lord, whose carnal and self-indulgent living shows no sign or record of His sanctifying touch. It is the task of Christians to clear the path to Him.

'Bring the boy to me,' said Christ, and there in five words is the divine commission for parents and teachers. It is an awful thought that we are the child's first image of God. I was overwhelmed and bowed my head in a prayer for help, when my daughter-in-law told me that my little grandson had asked her: 'Does God live at Titirangi?' Titirangi is the hill-suburb where we have our home. . . .

'Bring the boy to me,' said Christ, and we ourselves dare not approach that Presence unworthily. How humbly must we tread when we lead a child by the hand.

And so they brought the child to Christ. There is a note of hopelessness in the distracted father's voice: 'I asked your disciples to cast him out but they could not.' It is possible to catch the dull, flat tone of a disillusioned man. The chill of the impotence of those who should have aided him is on his heart even in the presence of the Lord: 'But if thou canst do anything,' he says without much hope, 'have mercy on us and help us.'

The Lord looked at him and said: 'If you can believe! All things are possible to one who believes.' At the words the man's heart caught fire. In days of doubt we should look steadily on His face. Turn the eyes on Him, and the world grows dim, the clutter of humanity falls away, and the heart grows strong. 'Lord,' he cried, 'I believe. Help my unbelief.' So the Authorized Version and Moffatt. 'I have faith. Help me where it fails,' Rieu renders. 'I do believe. Help me to believe more,' says J. B. Phillips. 'I have faith. Help me where faith falls short,' runs the New English Bible. Or translate: 'I believe, I believe, pity my faith's feebleness.'

So cried the poor man, and put a magnificent prayer into history. It is a prayer which, of all prayers, can claim an answer. The Lord demands no impossible coercion of mind or soul. He presents no list of man-made dogmas. He asks for no intellectual dishonesty, no vain words, or insincere profession. He asks us to look steadily in His eyes, and trust Him to be what He professed to be. He asks for a willingness to try, for the merest bridgehead in the soul. None can help the surge of doubt, but doubt need not be fostered and cherished, misnamed integrity of mind, and laced with pride and posturing.

A burning desire for God must lie at the core of all faith. Perhaps, in the mystery of God's ways with men, that is why faith saves. Doubt too often finds its origin in a half-suppressed desire not to believe, to find some way out of faith's stern obligations. The father in the story wanted blessing, and with that firm invincible desire beneath its feet faith found a place to kneel and then to stand.

It is those who hunger and thirst after righteousness who are filled. Few people in this affluent society understand the poignant power of that metaphor. I remember being thirsty once. Five years ago we were on the island of Delos in the Aegean with a party of classicists. The island lay brown and baked under the merciless August sun. No blade of grass, no green leaf broke the desolation. The land lay in the purple sea like a place accursed, a 'hissing and a desolation' in Jeremiah's phrase, burned brown in the pitiless sun, without a tree, a flower or a green blade of grass. The white ruins of a town and market-place lie on the island, hot marble and stone, where the merchants once lived who battened on the foul slave-trade of the Greco-Roman world. There is no one on the island today. We landed in the still morning, and there was not even the cry of a sea-bird to break the stillness of the death which lay on the old centre of man's inhumanity and cruelty.

We wandered through the ruins of streets, shops, and temples, shrivelled by the savage sun. We climbed the four-thousand-year-old stairway to the little peak of Cynthus, a five-hundred-foot pile of polished rock above the cave where legend said Apollo was born. Gasping in the heat, we found the imagery of the Bible come vividly to life, 'the shadow of a rock in a weary land,' the tree 'planted by the rivers of water.' The view was superb, the desolate circle of the isle, the sharp ruins of its town, the mauve circle of the Cyclades, and the incredible violet of the interweaving sea. But it was difficult to take an interest in the historic scene because of thirst. At the hill's foot, as we came down, some traders from Mykonos, whose humped mass lay to the west, were setting up their wares and selling drinks. Our party of classicists streamed past the little museum full of amazing objects of art, which had also been opened for our visit. None had any thought beyond thirst. I realized that day what thirst can be, a sharp, demanding pain. The Lord's audience knew thirst like that. Palestine lies in the same latitude. They knew hunger too as we have never known it.

'Blessed are they who hunger and thirst after righteousness.' As we walked through the dust to the jetty we asked ourselves whether we had ever desired righteousness with the intensity of our thirst on that August day, ever so longed to do His will, to be like Christ, with such a longing, so ardently that nothing matters beside, be it career, comfort, wordly success, prosperity, health, life itself. What could our Lord do with us if we truly thirsted to be like Him, 'to know Him and the power of His resurrection'? What could He do with a Church thus ardent in faith, hope, and love? That thought is the key to the rest of the story.

The Disciples' Impotence

We should turn back now to the scene below the hill before Christ, Peter, James and John returned. There is more in the story than Mark's brief narrative tells. Peter, after all, was not present, and Peter was Mark's authority. The story is full enough from the point of his arrival. The nine disciples were riding a wave of popular interest. It is easy enough to collect a crowd. Pathetic stunting in the Church often succeeds well enough in this trivial process. Hymns to jazz tunes, rock and roll, the twist in the parish hall, unscrupulous exploitation of prophecy, noisy attacks on this and that, will collect the curious. But to what end?

Note, too, that the scribes were there. The doctors of the law were interested in the prophet from Galilee and his men, and the disciples were not a little proud, and anxious to turn the situation to profit. Perhaps in their innocence they were out to impress the religious leaders with a notable miracle. But as the great James Denney once remarked: 'No one can bear witness to himself and Jesus Christ at one and the same time. No man can at one and the same time show that he himself is clever and that Christ is mighty to save.' 'How now, ye rebels,' shouted Moses, 'shall we bring water out of this rock?' It was disaster in his great career.

A man-made mass-movement is harmful. The exaltation of a person or an institution in empty religious excitement is lamentable. Christ is hidden, the way barred to His healing hand, when strutting self-important men advertise their sham religious wares before the multitude. Before man's real problems such mountebanks are helpless. Christ can work only through the humble, the devoted, the dependent. He chooses 'the weak things of the world' to do His work. The man who said those words was one of the most powerful intellects of his age, and God chose Paul of Tarsus because he wished to use the sharp clean tool of his great mind. But that mind had to be surrendered, conscious of its need, malleable in his hand. . . .

'Why,' they asked Him that evening, 'were we unable to heal the lad?' There is evil so powerful, He replied, that it can be defeated only by prayer and fasting, by prayer which touches the godlike note of pain, prayer which is the merging of the whole being with God's will, prayer which involves the whole life, in a determination to do all, be anything, give everything that God's purpose can be effected, and His name be glorified.

We spoke of the reality and relevence of Mark's Gospel, and the universality of its truth. How does all this relate to our personal experience? We have known the high slopes of fellowship. God has seemed near, faith easy, the battle won. Next week we face reality again and the godless world. We shall be a unit in the faceless mass. We shall stand in the crowded tube and pour with the multitude out of Cannon Street or Charing Cross. The old intractable problems of office, shop, factory, or classroom will rise to greet us, as enormous as ever. There will be no one to walk with by the lake in whom to confide the story of stress, tension, and injustice. There will be no like-minded multitude among whom to hide and feel protected and strong. It will be the lonely way again, the solitary conflict with despair. Remember then what the visit to Hermon was meant to teach. Remember the closer revelation of the glory of the Lord. Remember that you are not alone. We know little, indeed, of Christ, if the warmth of our discipleship depends upon the fellowship of others. Such fellowship is sweet, it is part of the blessing which Christ's service brings, but Christ is as real and near in the seeming loneliness, as truly present when the way is rough. On a tattered sheet of papyrus found in Egypt in the early years of this century was a saying of Christ: 'Break the stone and there thou shalt find Me; cleave the wood and there am I.' It seems to mean that the divine Presence is also theirs who work on the lonely roads, or as humble hewers of wood toil in the forests, the slaves, the rejected of the cruel world. Where two or three are gathered together there He is in the midst. And where men are burdened and alone there too He abides. Christ is in tomorrow.

With joy, therefore, we face the weeks to come. Few other than Christians can. . . .

> Tomorrow, and tomorrow, and tomorrow,
> Creeps in this petty pace from day to day . . .
> And all our yesterdays have lighted fools
> The way to dusty death . . .

So moaned the doomed Macbeth. There was no Christ in
his tomorrow, only emptiness, 'sound and fury signifying
nothing.' In Christ, our tomorrow is full of purpose.
Temptation will come no doubt, to self-pity. You know
how to deal with such invaders. Shall I give you as I close,
two quotations. In writing a Scripture Union note last
year, I found Moffatt's rendering of 1 Peter 4. 7: 'Steady
then. Keep cool, and pray.' The second quotation is longer,
some verses I found and wrote in the diary I took abroad
with me five years ago:

> Lonely? Look up!
>   Let the world grow dim;
> There is steadying strength,
>   When you journey with Him.
> Doubting? Fear not!
>   For the promise holds true,
> That the child of God's care
>   Shall his faith renew.
> So rested and steadied,
>   And nourished and stilled,
> Claim each promise of God,
>   And each need shall be filled.

THE MAN WHO TURNED AWAY

Mark 10. 17-31.

At some point in the journey there was a dramatic incident. Someone came running, forgetful of all dignity and kneeled impulsively in the dust. He was young, Matthew tells us, he held high office in the Jewish religious community, says Luke. All three evangelists who tell the story leave us in no doubt that he was a rich man, and by the common standards of society a blameless character. As Harold St. John puts it: 'he seemed to have all the keys of life hanging at his girdle—wealth, youth, prestige and a blameless character but withal an empty heart.'

The young man, as young men are, was conscious of his lack, restless and in quest of something which eluded him. Such divine discontent would make a sombre anthology from the world's literature. The French had a name for it in the days of their Romantic Movement. It was called *le mal de siècle*—'world-weariness' if you will, but it was neither French nor modern. The earliest Greek literature could be used to document it, and Roman poetry too. Sappho and Catullus could stand side by side. Youth early discovers that the brave new world is not built of carnality, comfort, success, material possessions. There is an elusive element. The missing factor is found only in God.

'Good Master'

The young man in the story caught a glimpse of this truth. The discovery stirred him to the depths. Here on the road with his band of disciples was the One who could help

him. He cast reserve and respectability aside, ran, and
kneeled. 'Good Master,' he cried, 'what must I do to win a
part in eternal life?'

In this illuminating story several points must be noted.
The first is the unwillingness of Christ to take advantage of
a state of emotional excitement. Christ's followers, likewise, should take care not to use mere emotion to secure
decision. Both heart and brain, as Housman once remarked,
can mislead:

> Oh my two troubles, they reave me of rest,
>   The brains in my head, and the heart in my breast. . . .

The brain, none the less, is the senior partner in the complex
of personality, and if not given the first word, is liable to
have the last. Decision made in a mood of emotional excitement is not soundly based and is liable to reversal. Hence
post-revival tragedies.

Abiding conviction must be based on reason. It must
count first the cost of decision. It must follow calm and
deliberate choice. Christ saw that the youth kneeling in the
road was overwrought. He was not himself. He proceeded
to strip the self-deception away. '*Why* do you call me
good?' he asked. The emphasis, observe, is on the interro-
gative. The question was no disclaimer of goodness. He
paused, and prompted the silent young man. '*Why* do you
call me good? . . . There is no one good but God.'

The right answer lay ready. 'Master, have I not heard
what one of your men said yonder under Hermon? "Thou
art the Christ," he told you, "the Son of the Living God."
And have I not heard that you accepted the word? I call you
good because I know that you are the Messiah. I call you
good because God is good, and you have said that you and
He are one. This is no courtesy tag as I might use it to any

rabbi of the synagogue. I call you good because you are my Saviour. To my Saviour, the Messiah of Israel, I address my question. What must I do to inherit eternal life?'

On such a foundation the Lord might have built. All Christianity must begin with the recognition of the Lordship, the deity of Christ. There is no Christianity with a Christ who is less than God. A saint, a martyr, might inspire and daunt us. They could not save. In such a Christ alone we have eternal life. The young man might have had his answer there and then, but failed to grasp the truth.

The Law

There is a dramatic pause after verse eighteen. Picture the scene. The Lord, the well-dressed young man on his knees, with puzzled face uplifted. . . . The disciples, perhaps the village crowd, stand silently around. Life sometimes pauses there for all of us as we confront Christ with the eyes of the world upon us. Here is a challenge, and are we to rise to it? We are caught with a question. Are we to answer it?

The young man failed to reply. The Lord, still determined not to by-pass the will and clear conviction of the inquirer, turned to the old familiar pathway of the Law. He quoted the fifth to the ninth commandments, adding 'defraud not,' a precept from Deuteronomy (24. 14) referring to prompt payment of an employee's wages, and doubtless relevant in the case of a man with a large establishment.

Again the young man might have replied correctly. Had he conceived the Law aright, in the terms perhaps of the Sermon on the Mount, or in the manner which provided, a generation later, some of the most passionate confessions of Paul, he would have replied: 'Master, I know the Law, and have sought as long as I can remember to meet its demands and to fulfil it. All I find is despair and frustration. The Law does not save me from sin, it merely underlines my sin. There is a Law in my members warring against the Law of my mind. I need not a code but a Saviour. Be merciful, Lord to me, a sinner.'

He said none of this. The puzzled face looked up. 'Master, I have done all these things.' The Law had not done its work of conviction in him. He had confused respectability with goodness. Morality for him was passive, a mere abstaining. It was not active, a drive to do. The pity of it. We all know such people and covet them for Christ, but their sheer blamelessness in the accepted sense, is a barrier between them and Him. The Lord 'looked at him and loved him.' There is yearning in the phrase, and His longing to break through and make the self-satisfied youth see and understand how shallow was the outer rectitude which he so prized.

Moment of Truth

In Christ's dealing with men there comes, as we saw in a previous chapter, a recognition, a moment of truth. It is possible sometimes to see Him precipitate that moment. The woman at the well of Sychar fenced with Him on matters of theology, and suddenly He broke her confidence, and silenced her vain sparring of words by telling her: 'Go call your man.' She rose to that occasion, confessed the barrenness of the life she had sought to conceal, and found salvation.

A similar moment comes with Verse Twenty-one. It contains a devastating challenge. 'You have said that you defraud no one. Very well. Go and sell all your goods, give it all to the poor, and follow me.' The words must be set in their context. The Lord demanded no such absolute sacrifice from the comfortable little household in Bethany. He cannot have meant that mere possessions were themselves evil, and a barrier in the way of a man's salvation. It must have been a special case. Here was a man who calmly said that he had met all his obligations to society. This was in Palestine, probably one of the hungriest and most poverty-stricken corners of the Empire. Awful want was clamant around, and yet one young man contrived to hold and to enjoy great possessions. No doubt he paid his tithes with care and precision, gave the due amounts the Law demanded, and fulfilled all formal obligation. It had never occurred to him that there was cruel incongruity in his great wealth and the misery of his neighbours. Possessions possessed him. His wealth was the most important feature of his life, and the Lord demonstrated this with a clarity which overwhelmed him. He wanted what he described as eternal life. In the final analysis it was shown that he preferred this life. It is a test, let us admit it, which few of us would like to face.

It broke the young man. He rose, turned away, and left with downcast eyes. Looking after him, and turning to His disciples the Lord said: 'How difficult it is for those who have riches to enter into the Kingdom of God.' The word in the Greek text is *chremata* which also means 'things.' The root is that of the verb 'use,' and fundamentally *chremata* are 'useful things.' Wealth, in other words, is what we can use, and it follows that wealth is what we should use. It was the fault of the unprofitable servant in the Parable of the Talents that he hid away the money he had, and denied it useful employment. So it must have been with the young man in the story. His 'useful things' were denied their usefulness because they had taken the character of a soul that was dull and barren, and fired by no generosity or love.

F

And yet Christ loved him, perhaps for the spark of that day's desire. perhaps with a wider pity than we, His followers, can feel.

Trust in Things

Seeing the bewildered looks around Him the Lord amplified and explained His words, 'How difficult it is for those who trust in riches, who place their confidence in material things, to enter into the Kingdom of God.' The limits of wealth are apparent to every man and woman alive. The precious things of life cannot be bought. Love cannot be bought. Happiness, as Charlotte Brontë remarked, is not a potato which can be bought in a shop. Even health in the last analysis, cannot be bought. Friendship, love's lesser brother, is as elusive.

Dickens has a conversation between Mr. Dombey, the harsh, cold man of wealth, and his little son Paul, a tiny wisp of a boy, dying of leukemia, as we now can diagnose his case. 'Papa,' said Paul, as they sat by the fire, 'what is money?' Mr. Dombey was in a difficulty. He could hardly talk of bank-balances, rates of exchange, inflation and depreciation, currency and so on. He looked down at the little chair and answered: 'Oh, gold, silver, copper, sovereigns, shillings and so on. You know what they are?'

'Oh, yes, I know that,' said Paul. 'I don't mean that. I mean what is money after all? What can it do?' 'Money, Paul,' said Mr. Dombey, pompously, 'can do anything.' 'If money is a good thing, and can do anything,' said Paul looking into the fire, 'I wonder why it didn't save me my mother?' Mr. Dombey recovered from his surprise, almost his alarm at such lack of confidence in wealth. He explained that money caused its possessor to be honoured, feared, respected, courted and admired, that it made one powerful

and glorious in the eyes of men, and how it could even keep
death at bay for a long time. . . . Mr. Dombey spoke with
emphasis and Paul kept on looking into the fire. His little
dying face was very serious. He said: 'Money can't make
me strong and well either, can it Papa?' Nor can it a century
later for those who carry white death in the blood as little
Paul Dombey did. Things are manifestly not to be trusted
with what matters most in life.

Hence the saying which follows: 'It is easier for a cable to
go through a needle's eye, than for a rich man to enter into
the Kingdom of Heaven.' 'Cable,' note, not 'camel'. Ad-
mittedly the East is given to hyperbole and extravagance of
imagery. In the Talmud, an elephant passing through the
eye of a needle is twice used for that which is impossible,
and Christ Himself spoke elsewhere of legalists who 'strain
out a gnat' from their drinking-water, and 'swallow a
camel.' The West, however, does find difficulty in such
figures of speech, and one ingenious explanation of un-
known authorship maintains that the Needle's Eye was a
small postern-gate into Jerusalem. A camel could get
through either on its knees, or with its load removed, or
both. The edifying picture emerged of the rich man reach-
ing the Kingdom of God after appropriate humbling or
jettisoning of wealth. Shakespeare had heard of this explanation. 'It is as hard to come,' he says in *Richard the
Second*, 'as for a camel to thread the postern of a needle's
eye.' Unfortunately for this pretty explanation there is no
evidence for the existence of such a gate. Moreover Mark
uses a familiar word for needle. Luke uses quite another
word. Perhaps he used a medical term. Had there been a
gate called the Needle's Eye, one word only would have
been used for it.

The true explanation is in the Greek lexicon for anyone

to find. It has passed unobserved because it is located not under the word *kamelos*, which assuredly means 'camel', but under *kamilos* which means a hawser or ship's cable. In the Greek of New Testament times, the second language of the Middle East, the vowels were already passing through the process which, in Modern Greek, has made most of them sound like 'i'. Consequently *kamelos* and *kamilos* sounded very much the same. 'Camel' and 'cable', 'horse' and 'hawser' could similarly be misheard if someone was dictating in English to a roomful of copyists.

The Lord, of course, was speaking in Aramaic. The retreating figure was almost out of sight on his way back to the things in which he trusted. Christ said: 'It is easier to thread a hawser through a needle than to bring a rich man to complete reliance on God.' If a sermon is sought in the hawser it is there. The hawser will go through the needle's eye—if it is sufficiently stripped down.

Neutrality of Things

Things in themselves are neutral. They are neither good nor bad. It is how they are used which gives them character, and what they express. Science can be used for good or evil. A guillotine is used in printing works to cut paper. It was invented to sever heads. Silver can buy bread. In the hands of Caiaphas and Judas it was the price of Christ's betrayal.

Things, wealth and all else take the stamp and character of those who possess them. Here is an illustration. I once had half an hour to look at the vast archaeological museum in Athens. Instead of hurrying through gallery after gallery and coming away with a chaotic impression, my wife and I decided to spend a quarter of an hour with the lovely Vaphio cups, and a quarter of an hour with the gold masks from Mycenae.

These masks are death masks. Gold, of which the Mycenaeans had an abundance, was beaten out paper thin, and then pressed over the faces or the bodies of the dead before burial. There was a pathetic gold cast of a baby's body. The tiny prince had been put away in the earth wrapped in beaten gold. The little body was gone. The gold, remained. The masks possess strange power. Some of their shaping was the work of the artist, but there is small doubt that their character depended principally upon the face of the dead on to which the gold leaf was pressed and moulded. Schliemann, the great archaeologist, thought that one of the masks showed the dead face of Agamemnon, the royal commander of the Greeks, who was murdered treacherously by his wife on the night he returned from Troy. The mask is strangely powerful. It shows the face of a mature man set in a last look of agony. All the bitterness and pain of death at the moment of victory are stamped upon it. After three thousand years the visitor can stand before the glass case and see the face of a man who died shockingly at the blow of his wife's axe in the bath of his own palace.

But catch my meaning. The gold takes the character of the man it enfolded. His personality is impressed on the lifeless, neutral thing. On another mask is the thin-lipped impress of a man who seemed to smile sardonically at death, a man with secrets who fought death itself, and went down undefeated. It is the same gold, the same thin beaten sheet of yellow metal. Personality is the force which marks it.

So with all possessions. They take our shape and form, they mould themselves to our person, and reflect our character. Things bear the stamp of their possessor's consecration or rebellion, his worth or worthlessness. 'It is only Christian men" said Chesterton, "who keep even heathen things.' Nothing is safe from corruption, misuse, abuse in godless hands.

But note, too, that possessions give greater scope for expression. In good or evil hands they seem to make the good or evil more visible, more potent, more rich in usefulness or damage. Things have triumphed in this affluent society. Man is rich. Never has man expressed himself so arrogantly and visibly. The Pharaohs built the pyramids which still defy the battering of time. The vast stone of the Coliseum still holds the evil of imperial Rome. But can any vision of human dominance equal the uplifted cliffs of the skyscrapers of Lower Manhattan, seen from the water? Poverty is not obtrusive. Wealth is, because wealth gives man wide scope to reveal himself. Hence, too, it tempts to display, offers chance and opportunity to pride and insolence, to selfishness and arrogance which in humbler circumstances might lie dormant in the soul.

Basically what the young man who came to Christ would not face was self-abandonment. His demonstration of humility was as formal as his address to the Lord. He was asked to let go that which had become his chief concern and preoccupation. No man can truly follow Christ who is not willing to put Christ first.

His wealth passed away. Before his life was ended the rich young man, elderly now, saw flame and destruction sweep through Palestine. He saw crops trampled, olives cut down, farmhouses flaming. If he possessed property in Jerusalem he saw it calcined by the Romans' fire. He might have better used it all while it could bear the stamp of love and pity, and a heart warmed by Christ. Walking down the road, with his back to Christ, the rich young ruler is a sight for tears. He knew about money, all about prices, but his values were all wrong. There was another man, unnamed, who found his way into a tiny parable of Christ. He found a pearl of great price and sold all that he had to possess it. Peace in God, a knowledge of sins forgiven, fellowship with Christ, the manifold blessings of home, of love, of courage, confidence, and care, which accompany such a faith, are worth more than anything else in the world. We do well to let nothing stand in the way of our winning them.

CLIMBING WITH CHRIST

Mark 10. 32-45.

THE Passion of Christ began, not in the Upper Room, nor under the olives in the Garden of Gethsemane, but far down the road from Jordan. In Mark's Gospel the fact is unusually clear. Phillips translates 10. 32: 'They were on their way going up to Jerusalem, and Jesus walked on ahead. They were puzzled and bewildered at this, but went on following Him with fear in their hearts.' 'They were awestruck,' says Weymouth's rendering. 'They were filled with awe,' says the New English Bible. Moffat is wrong. His rendering, 'they were in dismay,' misses the finer meaning.

There was something strangely different about the mood of the Lord, and His men, obtuse in so much, noted it with awe. What is awe? It is, says the Oxford English Dictionary, 'a solemn and reverential wonder, tinged with latent fear, inspired by what is sublime and majestic.' There was a deep change in their Master, which the disciples could not miss. Luke, describing the same scene, remarks that, 'He set His face steadfastly to go to Jerusalem.' 'He made His face firm,' says the Greek text, as though to meet something formidable and unwelcome.

But Mark's account, with Peter's realistic words behind it, catches the tense emotion of the occasion best. The commentators in various languages have noted it. They speak of 'majesty and heroism' in Him who led the way. He stepped out *more intrepidi ducis*, 'like a dauntless leader,' says Augustine; *mutig und entschlossen*, 'valiant and resolved,' says the German.

Indeed He laboured under strong emotion. Memory mingled with expectation. In the villages of the Ten Towns, He had instructed His men, and sought to fortify them for the coming ordeal. And now the ordeal was visible along the road. All the strength of a perfect and sensitive manhood revolted from the horror, agony, and degradation which He knew awaited Him in the harsh cruel city, which had 'killed the prophets, and stoned them which were sent to her.' The end loomed, and it was still possible to take the easy road and escape the Cross. He won that battle, but not without emotion.

Upward Way

Let us look at the sublime Figure, striding on. His is always the upward way. His path never leads down, and to follow Him in never effortless or cheap. It is a path that is often lonely and misunderstood. His very friends were 'puzzled and bewildered'. The world is baffled still, and not infrequently scornful and angry at the Christian's upward striving. It demands something of His resolution to follow, His obedience, His readiness to pay the price in 'blood and sweat and tears', His loneliness at times, His utter self-control. It calls for His clarity of purpose and fixity of goal. 'Easy is the way down to the world of death,' runs one of the best-known lines in Vergil, 'day and night the door of the Nether King stands open: But to call back the step, and emerge to the upper air, there is the task, and there the toil.'

The most sensitive of Roman poets had caught a truth in his lines. To slide into the mass is easy. To drift with the tide, conform, give in, follow the crowd, demands no effort. To obey Paul's precept, and 'be not conformed,' or, as Phillips renders it, to prevent the world from 'forcing us

into its mould', calls for all the Christlike valour of the
Christian soul. He always strides ahead. His way always
ascends.

Those Who Followed

There were others beside Christ on the Jerusalem road.
They, too, were on their way to a great time of testing, but
unlike their Master, were unaware of the need for solemn
preparation. Perhaps it says something for them that, in
puzzle and bewilderment, they still followed. Sometimes
our following is little more than the momentum of habit.
There is some virtue in such automatism. When we fly
blind and wearily, there is usefulness in a mechanical pilot
which takes over and keeps the craft on course. But such
progress cannot be permanent. There must be conscious
direction, and conscious direction the disciples lacked.

Their goal was obscured. For all His instruction, they had
lamentably misunderstood their Lord. They still had their
eyes full of an earthly Kingdom, some material realm under
a new David, in which they, the perceptive and the faith-
ful, would inherit power. On this last journey, when the
humanity in the Lord desperately needed sympathy, understanding and fellowship, they all failed Him, as truly as
those whom He had especially prepared on the Mount of
Transfiguration failed Him in the last watch under the
olives of Gethsemane.

They were no team, no band of brothers that day, but a
divided group of self-seeking men. Nothing more awe-
somely demonstrates the patience of Christ than His response to James and John. He had taken them apart at some
hour of rest by the roadside, and quietly told them again
what awaited at Jerusalem, betrayal, pain, death, and resurrection. As though the words of direct solemn import had

made no impression at all, the two brothers came with a selfish and ambitious request. Could they sit on either side of Him in the day of His power? Without anger, without scorn, He answered them with careful sadness, gently disposing of their untimely selfishness. 'The only-begotten Son, He has revealed Him,' runs John 1. 18. In other words, in Christ we see God, a fact central in Christianity, and persistently forgotten by the arrogant theologians of the most recent modern vintage, who seek to rehabilitate our 'image of God.' We have our image of God, one God-given. In Christ we see God's love, God's wrath—and God's patience. If this was the patience of God, this quiet reply on the road near Jericho to the two shallow, self-seeking young men, there is hope for our stupidity and failure to apprehend.

On that climb, the leader needed trustful and trusty companions, but they were bad climbers. They pulled the rope to aid themselves, and made a heavier burden on His strength and courage, dragging on their leader, without clear consciousness of where He went and why. Are we much better? In retrospect, with the New Testament before us, and the whole clear plan open to view, it is easy to censure the obtuseness of the disciples. A sterner test is to transfer the story to the modern road, the same Christ, but another Jerusalem. Let us look at 'the Christ of the modern road,' to adopt the title of a controversial book of the 'Twenties.

Christ always moves ahead, outstripping His laggard followers, His objective clear before. What was one of His objectives for this decade? Without doubt, I think, revival. Evangelism, of the sort I thought had died with Moody and Torrey, came back with Graham, came with sanity, acceptance, and a fine unity among the churches. The old liberalism had demonstrated its impotence in empty pews

and disillusionment. Nor was a new and irreproachable
mass evangelism the only sign of the times. Orthodoxy had
begun to demonstrate its scholarship. Conservatism could
no longer be dismissed as obscurantism and the old-
fashioned prejudice of ignorance.

Opportunity confronted the Church, a new unity of
evangelical Christians, a new spirit of sympathy and co-
operation among those who had reached an impasse in
lesser interpretations of the Gospel, and had begun to think
wistfully that a purged and scholarly evangelical Church
was after all a refuge for both mind and soul. Christ
stepped ahead on a new road. What of his followers?

The great revival which could have come to this tense
and chastened generation has proved a mirage. Disrupted,
distrustful, pursuing petty prejudice and sectional ambition,
the band which might have followed, ardent, united, and
effective, has fallen apart. A neo-pentecostalism has
seduced the emotional and alienated the thoughtful, dissi-
pating spiritual energy in unseemly demonstration. A neo-
Calvinism has begotten an inverted pride, and a distrust of
evangelism as Arminianism, 'easy-believism', and a too
facile way to God. In such prejudice a strong and valuable
section of the Church has retired to an ivory castle, no
longer stirred by salutary concern, for 'will not God add as
God wills?' A neo-fundamentalism has equated orthodoxy
and faithfulness with forms of patriotism, forms of sectarianism, with resistance to Communism, with unceasing
controversy, and personal bitterness. In the process those
who grope back towards the truth are alienated and
shocked, and thrust away by tests of faith without foundation in Scripture.

On the Jerusalem road the band of those who follow has
fallen apart. The rest, we read, were angry with James and

John. James and John have angered the rest again, and in varied and complex patterns of envy, distrust and resentment, the followers of Christ have lost view of the great objective, failed to realize the reality of opportunity, and bewildered the world. The latest woe is the emergence of a new theism. Perhaps Christ is not the leader after all. Perhaps He only groped and sought like the rest. God is 'the core of love' in every one of us, neither outside us, outside time, outside the universe. In such mystic hopelessness is the last death of faith. Had the band moved on with Christ, revival might have presented the generation with a purged faith, and a Christ so relevant and real that men would seek no further.

The Personal Call

But consider this also. Anyone among the disputatious band on the road up from the Jordan could have abandoned lesser company and walked out ahead with Christ. Stepping on before, He found loneliness. In the same determination the Christian finds his Lord, and shares in the fulfilment of a plan. Preoccupation with lesser purposes holds us back from that full fellowship; half-heartedness, and lack of understanding do the same.

Perhaps we can find an illustration in the geography of this solemn story from Mark's Gospel, an illustration which has occasionally made a metaphor as we have considered it. 'His way always ascends' . . . 'They pulled on the rope, dragging on their leader. . . .' 'They went up to Jerusalem. . . .' A Bunyan might make another Pilgrim's Progress on the theme, with Christian living set forth as a task of mountaineering.

The Lake District, according to those who love and know it, is a paradise for rock-climbers. In that arduous sport I find no attraction. I have no head for heights, and a deep respect for the force of gravity. But there are athletic folk who find fascination in conquering the crags, and in his charming book, *Inside the Real Lakeland*, A. H. Griffin hás much to say, both practical and mystical, about rock-climbing. Its principles curiously illustrate the thoughts our theme suggests.

A man can hardly be half-hearted about any sort of mountaineering. The task calls for whole-hearted dedication of character, and a goal no lower than the top. It demands a cool and lonely courage, for many a problem must be worked out alone. It must have self-discipline, and the steady testing of each grip and foothold. Thoughtlessness is perilous on a high cliff-face, and rash haste can precede a fall. How true is all this to Christian living, to the task of climbing up with the valiant Christ.

The stark simplicities of the mountain crag bring the climber face to face with the moral law which is woven into the texture of Creation. 'You cannot afford to lose your temper, break your word, or act a lie on a difficult climb,' says Mr. Griffin. The climber is one of a team, and the team is roped together. Folly, deceit, fear, failure are transmitted down the rope. So, too, in the Church. Each person is part of a whole, harmed by another's fault, enriched by another's courage.

The chapter I quote from the Lakeland writer is almost a sermon on Bunyan's Hill Difficulty. But call it rather Life. 'Learn the rules,' says the author, 'and join a club.' There could be no better precept for Christian living. The ancient textbook is tried and tested. The 'Club', to be sure, has its faults, too evident to the watching multitude; there is dead wood in its member-list; but the Church cannot be by-passed by the follower of Christ.

'Know your limitations,' says Mr. Griffin, 'there is nothing clever in falling, and it can be a disgrace.' There is cool sense in that for our allegory. Peter did not realize his limitations when he boasted loudly of loyalty and faithfulness, and when he sought the comfort of the coal fire in the High Priest's courtyard amid hostile company which proved too much for his courage and steadfastness. 'Don't flaunt your ironmongery in the villages,' the climber continues, 'hide it in your rucksack.' Peter had flaunted his confidence: 'Though all the rest betray you, yet will I not.'

The Lakeland author concludes his climbing chapter with a sentence which makes one pause. The climber who conquers a peak, has conquered 'not the rock-face, nor the mountain, but himself.' How true is that of all victorious living. There are those who win the world, and lose their own immortal souls, who dominate families, underlings, even peoples, and remain the slaves, prisoners, and puppets of passion, carnality, and vice. The sublimest conquest is self. The majesty of the Master, stepping out ahead on the Jerusalem road, was the royalty of One perfectly governing self, and fully surrendered to the will of the Father.

Everest of the Spirit

But is not the walk with Christ a walk which shares His peril and His sacrifice? Indeed it is. They asked for a place on His right hand and on His left when He came into His Kingdom. Ironically He 'came into His Kingdom' on the cross, and 'on His right hand and on His left' hung two thieves. If we would reign with Him we must also suffer with Him. To have part in His joy demands participation in His sorrows. The Everest of the spirit, like the great Himalayan peak, must be conquered by sweat and toil, by perilous ridge, deep crevasse, precipice and sliding snow.

But let us return, in conclusion, to the bare words of Scripture, and the original picture of Christ striding on alone. Had they moved up and walked with Him what might they have heard? Such conversation as they heard who sat with Him on the Mount, or walked with Him into the setting sun on the road to Emmaus, such teaching as that which He wove round the sculptured vine on the evening of the arrest, in the Temple courtyard, such revelation as He built into His comment on the stones of the same Temple. And all this in place of the petty quarrelling and bickering which occupied them in the rear. Is a home cursed with tension, bitter words, bad temper and irritation? Move up and walk with Christ. Is a friendship demeaned by gossip, traffic in scandal, conversation which dishonours and debases? Move forward and talk with Christ. With Him is the place of enlightenment.

And it is the place where we realize ourselves. Behind, at a safe, or should we not rather say, a dangerous distance, they spoke of position and advantage, exalted their petty notions of honour, rights, authority, and built-up self-importance. Close to Him, they would have felt small and soiled, and then, as self surrendered, strangely washed and clean. With Christ is the place of conviction, and of cleansing. In paradoxical consequence the place of peril by His side becomes for those who choose it, the place of surest safety, for nothing little, unclean, mean, malicious, selfish or bare can live in that proximity. 'He that is near Me is near the fire,' runs a saying of the Lord, reported by Origen, and the word is no less than true. If, indeed, those words are from Christ, they are a reference to a prophecy of Malachi: 'Behold, I will send my messenger, and he shall prepare the way before me: and the Lord whom ye seek shall suddenly come to his temple . . . but who may abide the day of his coming? and who shall stand when he ap-peareth? for he is like a refiner's fire. . . .'

Were the words uttered when He cleansed the Temple? He stood, I think, in the courtyard with the knot of ropes, discarded from the cattle led to sacrifice, swinging in His hand. He did nothing, nothing at all, only stood and looked, for the Sadducees who ran the market in the Temple yard had no specific charge of assault to lay. He stood and looked, and the uneasy cattlemen wilted beneath His eye. Perhaps someone whispered the words of Malachi. Panic spread, and was caught by the beasts as beasts can catch the mood of man. Hence wild stampede and confusion amid the overturned tables. He burned like fire. He still does amid the grubbing and baseness of our lives. We can protect our sin only by protecting it from His nearness, His presence, His scrutiny. But what foolishness.

Let us rather stride out and join Him, bid Him burn the folly and evil out of us, fill our minds with His clean thought, make our lips speak His words, and grant us the fellowship beyond price.

With Him tension is purged from fellowship, selfishness from friendship, impurity from love, base motives from service, sin, in a word, from self, and self is merged in Christ.

Christ of the Upward Way,
   My Guide Divine,
Where Thou hast set Thy feet
   May I place mine;
And move and march wherever Thou
      hast trod,
   Keeping face forward up the hill
      of God.

G

THE HINGE OF HISTORY

Mark 11. 1-11; 15. 1-37; 16. 1-14.

These passages speak powerfully for themselves. A simple reading of Chapters Eleven to Fifteen of Mark's Gospel, with no introducing comment, might be more poignant and more potent than any exposition of the text. But a sermon can fulfil a purpose if it can turn the hearer back to Scripture with deeper perception and understanding. This Chapter has no other object.

The scene in old Jerusalem is no unfamiliar story from a strange and alien world. Here is man, and here is history. Let me illustrate. In the forest-filled valley behind my home lay an ancient *kauri* log, the remains of a splintered tree abandoned by the pioneer timber-snatchers of a century ago, when they greedily devastated the hills in quest of the glorious golden wood of the great *kauris*. There was much good firewood in the old log under the trees which have grown and hidden the cruel scars since the men with the axes and fire went their way, so we put a deep saw-cut in its middle. There, revealed in the hundreds of growth rings, was the history of the land, its changing seasons, its cycles of weather. You could count back to the days of Captain Cook, when no city spread across the isthmus. You could count back further still.

But mark this. The record ran right through the log. The same rings could have been read in the rotted stump across the little stream, where the great tree once stood in majesty. The same rings ran up to the spreading crown of branches which once topped the straight clean bole. We cut in one place, and revealed what was true below and above. The story of Christ's Passion is like a cut in history. It shows what had always been true of man. It shows what remained true. It shows what is still true.

The Crowd was the Same

Crowds have always been the same. A few short days before they had yelled acclaim as Christ rode into Jerusalem. He deliberately fulfilled a well-known prophecy that day. Zechariah had said: 'Rejoice greatly, O Daughter of Zion. Shout, O Daughter of Jerusalem. Behold thy King cometh unto thee. He is righteous and victorious, lowly and riding upon an ass.' There was no compromise in his offer of Himself. He never comes to man on any other terms than His own, nothing less than Lord and Saviour, a Risen Christ who will lay burning hands on cherished sin. Then, as now, the multitude was willing to accept Him on their own terms. Here was the descendant of their ancient line of kings, an ally against the proud collaborating priests, a rallying point for their hatred against Rome, someone to fire pride, exclusiveness, national self esteem. They had then discovered that He had no plans for their personal advantage, he offered no tribute to their pride, that there was to be no blaze of vengeance on the foreigners they hated, and the upper-class collaborators whom they loathed. He was no leader of the masses. Indeed He called for love, forgiveness, reconciliation, readiness to suffer, from those who followed Him. And at that realization, enthusiasm turned to contempt, and their spite was poured on the One Who had disappointed them and their base ambitions.

In other words they were a very human crowd in the Jerusalem streets. Sir John Sheppard, the Cambridge classical scholar, once challenged my use of the word 'human' in that sense. I do, however, insist that there is a sombre colouring in the adjective which sometimes fits the dark occasion. I mean that the crowd who called for the death of Christ was not composed of monsters, they were not picked for special wickedness. They were a fair sample of humanity, and that allegation is not easily put aside. Some- one has recently told of an audience in a Congo college viewing a film on the trial of Christ. As the rough soldiers thrust and jostled the silent Figure in the barracks room and crushed the crown of thorns down over His brow, the cry arose, '*Pika! Pika!*' which means, 'Hit Him! Hit Him!' In unbelieving horror those who showed the film realized that those who watched were not by any means on the side of the sufferer. They despised the unresisting Christ. They were declaring for violence, strength, for beating down the weak. '*Pika! Pika!*' 'Crucify! Crucify!' And lest you dis- miss such a reaction as a product of the jungle, I shall re- mind you that the vaster cruelties of our day were not in- vented in the jungle. It was not in Central Africa that naked Jews with babies in their arms were driven into long pits to be shot. Brain-washing was not invented in the primitive forest, nor the gas-chamber, nor the agony of the Arctic labour camp. Plato, the greatest mind among the Greeks, viewing steadily his Athenian contemporaries, the most cultured race in the ancient world, said calmly, four centuries before Christ, that he supposed that, if the truly good man ever appeared on earth he would be tortured and rejected, and in the end crucified. So it happened, and so it happens every day when any Pontius Pilate tries to wash his hands of duty, when any crowd clamours for evil, for injustice, and for blood. The principles of passion and sel- fishness on which that crowd made its choice, are those which determine action in a thousand contexts today. There is the same rejection of goodness and purity, the same utter carelessness for the unborn, the same contempt for others, for the future, the same clamour for wrong. They are too much like us for our comfort.

People are the Same

But take the crowd apart, and look at the men and women of that awful day. They are shockingly recognizable. There is a haunting poem of E. J. Simpson, 'Evan John' as he called himself, describing a scene in a Jerusalem hotel. He was on leave in the Holy City during the war, and found the place where the Lord had died a moving experience. The scene in the luxurious hotel was so remote from the scenes of the New Testament, the people so different. But was it? Were they? And a veil seemed to fade, and he saw that nothing had changed. They were all there in the lounge, Pilate, Caiaphas, Herod. . . .

Here where they scourged You, blow on sickening blow,
Here where Your blood spotted the Path of Pain . . .
  A sleek little waiter to twiddle me in
  Through the roundabout doors which shut out the fresh air,
  Carpets to tread on, softer than sin,
  And, 'Yes, Sir', 'Your hat, Sir', 'The bar, Sir, is there'
  Stink of French perfume, and tunes from Kentucky,
  Bored Jewish band with a palm tree beside,
  Spoils of the world for the few, for the lucky,
  Heart of the world that is breaking outside.
Here where the nails held fast the rending flesh,
While Death through the darkened hours creeps slow, too
    slow. . .
  Herod from Egypt with corn and with cotton,
  Held from the children till prices increase,
  Young Pontius Pilate with gleaming Sam Browne,

Sipping pink gin as he passes the buck:
'I've washed my hands of it, turned the job down,
'Tisn't my pidgin, if things come unstuck.'
Oh, You who felt the blood, the nails, the blows,
Pardon us now, as once you pardoned Rome
. . . .
And breathe o'er us who have forgotten you
Your ancient Peace—'They know not what they do.'

Yes, Pontius Pilate. Let us turn the light on him for a
moment. He is a familiar figure. . . . Pilate was not an old
man. He could have been as young or not much older than
the Man he was called upon to judge, and He was thirty-
three. He had been in Palestine only two or three years, but
long enough to jeopardize his career by terrible administra-
tive blunders. The Jews were no easy people to govern.
To rule Palestine in the first century was like governing
Cyprus during the recent crisis. The atmosphere was tense
and brittle. The hate and nationalistic passion, which broke
out in the fire and blood of the Great Rebellion a generation later, was hot in the air.

Generally the Romans had treated the difficult Jews can-
nily and carefully. Pilate was fool enough to despise them,
and deliberately stir trouble. In the British Museum his
small coinage may be inspected alongside that of his pre-
decessors. In respect for Jewish prejudice it was the fashion
to adorn the copper coins of Palestine with ears of corn,
vine leaves, and other accepted Hebrew symbols. Pilate
stamped his coins with a pagan priest's staff of office, to
present his subjects with the daily insult of carrying a
heathen device in their purses.

Such arrogance was on a par with the rest of his policy.
He did what no governor had done before: when he
marched the garrison in to Jerusalem, he sent the standards in

at the head of the column—and the standards bore the emperor's image. And this was not the only occasion on which he desecrated the Holy City. Clumsily seeking to do honour to the emperor, he hung a set of portrait plaques dedicated to him in Herod's Jerusalem palace. He used a sacred temple fund to provide Jerusalem with a water supply.

The Jews did not endure such treatment lightly. Twice they petitioned the emperor. Their clever envoys had no great difficulty in convincing the dour Tiberius that his administrator in Palestine was risking revolt. The old man sent a sharp command to Pilate to abstain from his deliberate acts of provocation, and he was not a person to be treated lightly. Pilate's career, perhaps his personal safety, had been gravely compromised, when the subtle priests who had beaten him before sought to force him, and in the end succeeded in forcing him, to murder an innocent man, who had challenged their corruption.

Pilate was like multitudes of harassed men who are daily brought face to face with Jesus Christ, and what He represents, with their will fettered and action compromised by past folly and corruption. There is one course open to such men, and that course is at all costs to have done with past folly and corruption. The cost may be great, but there was a worse fate for the troubled Roman that day than loss of office, or even loss of life. It was more grievous than all loss to buy his immunity with innocent blood, and to be branded for ever as a coward and a betrayer of justice, to sell his soul for imaginary safety.

Christ is the Same

But now, as Pilate said, 'Behold the Man.' . . . We have looked at the Judge, tangled in his past, and selling his soul because he could not rise up like a man and say, 'Come death, come life, at all costs I shall follow the right.' . . . We have looked at the Crowd, taking its tone from its basest elements, choosing evil, and with it ruin, in the passion of the moment. . . . It remains to look at the Prisoner. It is a sight to overwhelm heart and mind. . . .

If you read the story in the Gospels carefully you will see that Jesus Christ had foreseen this moment. He came deliberately to Jerusalem, knowing that His enemies would wreak their will on Him. As you read, it is possible to see His mind moving through Old Testament scriptures which uncannily foreshadow the sufferings of a Servant of God. On the cross He quoted the Twenty-Second Psalm, with its strange and awful picture of one dying, pierced in hand and foot. At any time during the tense week in Jerusalem He could have withdrawn. Jerusalem and all its environs were fantastically crowded. A Roman governor once asked for a return of the number of animals sacrificed during the Passover week, and a Jewish historian, who was also the Emperor Vespasian's secretary, calculated on the figures given that Jerusalem's population rose that week to well over two million. The total seems almost incredibly large, but halve the figure, and it still suggests a thronging horde in which any resourceful fugitive could be hidden. It was impossible to police the crowds, and the Galileans among them, a notoriously turbulent element, would have rallied to support a man from their own district, had they been called upon.

The authorities were tense and anxious. They had not anticipated the popular support which they received from the mob in the street. Hence their anxiety to get it all over before morning. It is quite clear that even up to the time of His arrest, Jesus Christ could have escaped death. But He chose death. That is the astounding thought. After Judas had left the Supper, with Christ's command ringing in his ears, 'That which you do, do quickly,' the party was led by their Master to the Temple courtyard, where He discoursed with them on momentous matters. Then, when all was said which He desired to say, they all went to the Garden of Gethsemane where they were accustomed to spend the night. He went first to the Temple court because He knew He would be undisturbed there for the hour He needed. He went next to the Garden because He knew the traitor would seek Him there with the band of Temple guards. Could there be clearer indication that Christ knew what was to come and accepted it?

Look steadily at the Prisoner, for here was One of superb courage, choosing to die the most unimaginably horrible of deaths, because He saw in that surrender the fulfilment of a plan of God. His disciples saw only tragedy, but when on the third day He appeared again, risen from the dead, they saw that there was meaning in His death of supreme importance. It is strange to find the story of that glorious event so briefly recorded in the first Gospel to be written. True, Saint Paul had already written at length about it, for the First Epistle to the Corinthians was already circulating in the Church before Mark wrote.

But why the brevity? Time, perhaps, was short, and the writer's pen hasting to tell the tremendous ending to the Gospel before the moment of arrest. Like the Venerable Bede in the famous story, hastening to put the last verses of John's Gospel into English, Mark may have sped over his last chapter, his ear alert for the tramp of soldiers' boots on the flagstones. Indeed, he may have failed to finish, for there are a few curious verses at the end, which are perhaps by another hand.

But Mark knew the witnesses. Especially, he knew Peter, and in his Resurrection story, there is one touching and authentic echo of Peter's voice: 'Go your way,' says 'the young man' to the women at the tomb, 'tell his disciples *and Peter.*' This was a precious word for the wounded man. Again and again in the Gospel of Mark, we can see the traces of Peter's insistence that the truth about him be fully told. The story of Peter's betrayal is related with stern frankness, and it can have only been at Peter's express command that his son in Christ told the story in all its detail. It was left to John, thirty years later, to tell the full story of restoration, and the conversation with the Risen Christ on the beach.

Christ is still the same. He bids those who proclaim His Gospel tell the world that He is risen, to tell the world, *and you*, you who are beaten and defeated, and need above all things the confidence that He lives and loves; you who have taken like Peter the easy way out of temptation, and found the old evil things rise in power to reclaim the life, you who have sought the way back with tears, and have heard the horrible whisper that it is too late. You are in the message. Put your name where Peter's is, and go on in sure faith of forgiveness.

The Remnant are the Same

We have looked at two words in Mark's Resurrection story. Let us look at one word in the story of Calvary. It is profitable to look at detail in Scripture. Mark (15. 36), and he is echoed by Matthew, speaks of the offer of a sponge full of rough wine to the Lord just before His last moment of agony. The sponge, says the story, was uplifted on a stick, the 'reed' of the Authorized Version. There is a curious variant in John's account: 'They filled a sponge with vinegar, and put it upon hyssop, and put it to his mouth.' Now this would occasion no difficulty were it possible to produce a stick from a plant of hyssop, strong and long enough to hold a sponge full of liquid, and to be visible from the back of the crowd.

In point of fact it is not possible to do this. The hyssop is a bushy little plant, and not at all suitable for the purpose. But what if John wrote *hyssos* and not *hyssopos*? *Hyssos* means a spear, but is not a common word, and could easily have been changed by some early copyist to the better-known word. Indeed, one cursive manuscript does read *hyssos*. It is one of those emendations which, once one has seen it, one is convinced that it is correct. It is like the *kamilos* or ship's hawser, which cannot be threaded through a needle. How much more likely is this than *kamelos*, the poor camel which the ingenuity of commentators has been trying to fit into various needles' eyes ever since. John was there, by the Cross of Christ. He saw a soldier stick his spear into a sponge, dip it in the cruse of ration wine, which was provided for the detachment, and offer it to the Lord. Perhaps he heard the same soldier use the unusual word for spear, and included it in his text. Peter, who told Mark, and whom Matthew followed, was at the rear of the crowd, and all he saw was an uplifted stick.

But observe the situation. The crowd had engulfed ten of the Lord's disciples. Judas was wandering somewhere, a distracted fugitive, dogged and burdened by remorse. I suppose he could have burst through the cruel, mocking crowd and fallen at the foot of the Cross, and won forgiveness even at that ghastly thirteenth hour. But remorse held him, and drove him to receive in the Field of Blood the last wages of sin. One of the Twelve alone was in his proper place. John was with Mary at the side of Christ. That is why he reports so authentically the story of the javelin and the sponge of wine.

Note again. . . . So tenuous at this moment was the thread of God's vast purpose, that all the loyalty and open love He could command was that of three women and one young man. The man was not given any special revelation. No illuminating word broke the darkness for him. He was given one task to do, and he did it. He took Mary home. He could see only one step ahead. He saw that it was his duty to stand by the One he loved, and took his stand, facing fearlessly the rabid horde, and the hatred of the chief instigators of crime. He was shown one more step, and took it. He did the moment's duty. Sometimes we can do no more.

Surely, one might think, this done, all duty was done. But John did not stay with Mary in the safety of his lodging-place. He put her there, and went back. He thrust and elbowed his way through the crowd, as he had done when he extricated Mary, and returned to his place. Compare Mark's account with John's, and look at Matthew and Luke, and you will see strange omissions. John, escorting Mary, must have reached his awful station when his Master had already hung there some time in agony. He was soon dismissed to perform his work of mercy. He came back in time to record the last events. But he came back determined to do his duty to the bitter end.

Opportunity is Still the Same

Most surely we are somewhere in this story, and if we would have the benediction of the Lord, and know the truth in all its fullness, we must follow John to the Cross. In the crowd there is no blessing. Christ does not deal with crowds. They are the plaything of Antichrist. We have seen enough of the crowd this century, roaring sub-human slogans at Nuremberg with the great swastikas high over the platform, yelling for war in the Piazza Venezia, with Mussolini on the balcony, pouring in field grey across the frontiers, roaring revolution in Red Square.

Antichrist works through crowds, Christ deals with remnants and with men. All through the Old Testament, all through the New, the true men and women of God have been a few. Toynbee, the century's greatest historian, has shown that progress and leadership lies always in the hands of creative minorities. In the story of God's dealings with men this is most pre-eminently true. Crowds destroy and corrupt. Always know that something is wrong if you find yourself shouting with the mob. There was goodness, love, pity in Jerusalem, when they crucified Christ, but all goodness was smothered and helpless when it was lost in the mob.

To be effective, good must separate and stand apart. It is true today, as it was true then, that it is alone, and only alone, that a soul can find Christ. There is nothing for you, if you are lost in the multitude, conforming, coloured by their baseness, afraid to differ and to strive against the thrust and push of their downward movement and to stand apart. As you are today, so would you have been then. We have simply missed the historical situation, but that situation, as I have tried urgently to show, is of all time. The grain runs right through the tree. . . .

Where then, would you have been? With Judas, who turned bitter against love, because petty ambition or self seeking was frustrated? The embittered of all ages have sought to smash the society or the person which has caused their pain. And there are embittered men who have died in their bitterness, and failed to find the healing and assuagement which is found in Christ.

With Peter, lost and ineffective in the hostile, faceless horde? With the rest, unmentioned, unnamed in the story, because they found no place to stand on history's highest platform, at the turning hinge of all the ages? How vast the opportunity lost in timidity, disillusionment, or cowardly despair.

Or with John, the bravest of the brave? The path to the Cross lies where he showed it to be. It runs straight through the crowd, careless of their comment, obstruction, or suffocating pressure. It runs thither from any place, from any situation, from any sin, from any failure. It calls only for the will to rise, and thrust all opposition aside. To win the rich benediction of Christ you must somewhere, somehow reach that place, convinced that the Lord's self-chosen death is something relevant to our baseness, and passionately desiring, under the awful impact of that thought, to abandon the godless crowd, to stand with the Prisoner, to die, as it were, with Him, in order to live a new life with Him. Listen to what Paul wrote to the church in Rome. I shall read it in Phillips's translation, a modern version of the sort I suggested you should read: '. . . all of us who were baptised into Jesus Christ were, by that very action, sharing His death. We were dead and buried with him . . . so that just as He was raised from the dead . . . so we too might rise to life on a new plane altogether . . . let us never forget that our old selves died with Him on the Cross that the tyranny of sin over us might be broken.'

Epilogue

And so we end Mark's little book. It is fast-moving, tense, and eager to convince. In this book I have used *about* Mark and his book four times as many words as Mark used *in* his book. I trust that the real message is not lost in a sea of words. If we have read the signs aright, the book was cut short at its vital ending. But the point was made. In a dying world, about to die himself, Mark proclaimed that Christ lived. One who could write thus under the darkening shadow of death must have known with utter certitude that Christ lived. He knew that the tomb was empty, and the gospel of a Risen Lord no deception of a defeated sect, no delusion of fervent enthusiasts, but literal truth.

Therein lies the 'full salvation' for which this movement and the great Keswick Convention have always stood. It is no passionate mysticism destined to be shattered at the first cold touch of mundane experience, no ideal, loved and longed for but mere frustration and disappointment in the midst of life's temptations, testings, and harsh trials. God intends us to be free from vicious faults, lurking fear, the bondage of sin. True, that blessed liberty too often eludes us, but it is our undoubted right in the Risen Christ. Could we but grasp with both hands of faith the truth of His eternal presence, nothing could defeat, daunt or destroy us. Victory, 'full salvation,' if you will, lies in the practice of His presence.

Christ lives, and if He lives, all our thoughts are open to Him, all our motives known, the gap between the true and the professed manifest, all our actions are visible, our difficulties felt, our failures pitied, all our endeavours seconded, our struggles aided. . . . I prepared this talk on a cold August evening by a log fire ten months ago. We lay under the shadow of a coming trial which made me tremble as I wrote the words I am uttering today. As I wrote this paragraph my wife read a passage from Moody's life, which so harmonized with the thought forming in my mind that I felt a strong surge of confidence and faith. For what was I trying to say? I wished somehow to put into clear, persuasive words the thought that such practice of Christ's presence does not make the personality remote, odd, and withdrawn from ordinary life. It produces no pale unhealthiness. . . . And from Moody's life these words were read to me as I sought language for that thought: 'He told me that he spent comparatively little time in secret prayer and had no experience of being weighed down and burdened before God. He did not try to get into this state. His work kept him in the spirit of prayer and dependence upon God, and he just gave himself wholly to the work.'

To live in Christ's fellowship is to live simply, safely, sanely, in quiet trust. Temptation withers in that companionship, pain becomes as meaningful as His, events assume proportion. Do not think I speak as one who never knows the power of evil. Like Paul I follow after, but I know that the truth lies where I say it lies, and to that place of rest, I strive. We are not alone. The Companion is real, sometimes stern, always uncompromising, infinitely loving, utterly true. In that realization lies full salvation, peace of mind, poise, heart's rest.